Life Anonymous

12 Steps to Heal and Transform Your Life

Kristin M. Snowden
Scott Brassart

ISBN 979-8-575-58691-3

Kristin
To my mom, my biggest cheerleader, whose absence is felt every day.

Scott
To my family, who loved me even when I was unlovable.

Contents

Acknowledgements

Kristin

There are many people whom I'd like to credit with inspiring and influencing this book, my career path, and my passions. First, I want to thank my co-writer, Scott Brassart. He brought clarity to my scattered thoughts and boosted my waning confidence. Without you, Scott, this book would still just be an idea buzzing in my head.

My family bore the burden of my unrelenting focus on this book. I am grateful to my husband, Michael, and my children, Gweneth, Presley, and Kellan, for all the love, safety, and security they've provided, allowing me the space to pursue my passions and grow in my professional life. My family and friends have also offered me similar safety and joy, along with a fair amount of humbling "opportunities for growth." Thank you for respectfully challenging me, tolerating me, and supporting me. And a special thank you to those friends and family who read early drafts of this book and provided helpful feedback and edits.

I want to give a fan-girl shout-out to all the academics who've inspired my personal and professional life: Dr. Rob Weiss, Dr. Brené Brown, Dr. Bessel van der Kolk, Dr. Daniel Siegel, Dr. Allan Schore, Dr. Stephen Porges, Fr. Richard Rohr, Nadia Bolz-Weber, to name but a few. They are thought leaders who are changing people's lives for the better.

To all of my clients: I love what I do and it's because of the people I get to work with. I'd like to think that my clients learn and grow from my assistance. However, I'm certain that I constantly learn and grow from working with them. I feel grateful to be a part of their journeys.

To Every Person in Recovery, Ever (and To Those Who Love Them): I admire and respect you all. Your stories inspire me daily. My hope is that this book will carry some of your light and message to others.

Scott

As with Kristin, there are countless people I must thank for inspiring and influencing this book. First and foremost, my uber-cool coauthor Kristin Snowden. Without her interest as a non-addict in working and learning from the 12 Steps—not to mention her boundless enthusiasm—this book would never have been written. I need to also thank my friends Robert Stone and Mark Cassle for reading an early draft of this manuscript and providing countless helpful suggestions.

I want to posthumously thank Bill W, Dr. Bob, and other founders of Alcoholics Anonymous for starting the world on a path of healing and recovery. Without them, there would be no such thing as 12-Step recovery, and my life would probably still be a gigantic mess. And who needs that, right?

Similarly, I need to thank my 12-step recovery buddies for keeping me on the straight and narrow (mostly), for allowing me to bounce my occasionally crazy ideas off of them, and for listening to my story and my theories on recovery over and over so I could eventually understand—truly understand—the things I was saying. Brent, Roger F., Dale, Mark, Mike, Roger P., and too many others to name; you have all made my life immeasurably better. I cannot thank you enough for that.

Lastly, I want to thank my personal and professional mentors—Dr. Rob Weiss and Dr. David Fawcett. Each day, I learn something new from you. Your experience, intelligence, creativity, and generosity have made me the person I am today. Thank you.

—Scott Brassart

The 12 Steps

1. We admitted we were powerless over alcohol [or drugs, sex, gambling, eating, shopping, etc.]—that our lives had become unmanageable.
2. Came to believe that a power greater than ourselves could restore us to sanity.
3. Made a decision to turn our will and our lives over to the care of God *as we understood God*.
4. Made a searching and fearless moral inventory of ourselves.
5. Admitted to God, to ourselves, and to another human being the exact nature of our wrongs.
6. Were entirely ready to have God remove all these defects of character.
7. Humbly asked God to remove our shortcomings.
8. Made a list of all persons we had harmed and became willing to make amends to them all.
9. Made direct amends to such people whenever possible, except when to do so would injure them or others.
10. Continued to take personal inventory, and when we were wrong promptly admitted it.
11. Sought through prayer and meditation to improve our conscious contact with God *as we understood God*, praying only for knowledge of God's will for us and the power to carry that out.

12. Having had a spiritual awakening as the result of these steps, we tried to carry this message to other alcoholics [or addicts], and to practice these principles in all our affairs.

A Brief History of the 12 Steps

The 12-step model was first published in 1939 by Alcoholics Anonymous in their book, *Alcoholics Anonymous* (sometimes referred to as "the Big Book"). The original intent was to create a structured path to help and support any person who wanted to stop drinking. Basically, the 12 Steps are a list of suggestions providing clear, actionable guides for a life free from addiction. The steps are typically used in conjunction with regular attendance and participation in 12-Step meetings.

While the 12-Step recovery model began with AA, it has expanded to nearly 100 organizations created to help people in need find recovery from a wide range of addictions, compulsive behaviors, and mental health problems. A few of the more well-known 12-Step groups include Narcotics Anonymous, Sex and Love Addicts Anonymous, Overeaters Anonymous, and Debtors Anonymous.

Most addiction treatment centers incorporate the 12-Step model into their treatment programs. Typically, "working a program of recovery" involves a combination of therapy, 12-Step meetings, self-help reading, connecting with others who are working to heal from similar issues, and implementing the 12 Steps.

Introduction

A Non-Addict (Kristin) Finds the 12 Steps

I found the 12 Steps in a way I think many people find them: lost, desperate, broken, and looking for answers. No, I wasn't drinking daily or using any kind of drug to shroud my pain. I wasn't gambling, in debt, or overeating, either. To most, I appeared high-functioning, well-educated, and stable. Yet on the inside I was scattered, rage-filled, and drowning in fear and shame. In short, I was miserable.

My descent into my personal "rock bottom" was a slow and insidious process that took a few years and several life-event gut-punches. It steadily and stealthily chipped away at who I thought I was. I considered myself strong, yet I struggled to come to terms with my mother's untimely passing. I thought I was loving and happily married, but an angry, judging woman showed up when there were problems in my marriage. I thought I was smart, yet I couldn't reason my way out of misery, despite my education and training. I thought I was successful, yet I was failing in my marriage, which was a particularly difficult pill to swallow as a child of divorce.

This was not the life I planned.

Looking back, I can see the chain of events that led me to my personal crisis. It started in my late 20s when I was blindsided by infertility issues (my first flavor of being totally helpless). After years of heartbreak, we joyfully welcomed our first child. In the following year, we were shocked by not only an immediate unexpected pregnancy, but my mother's terminal diagnosis of pancreatic cancer. We moved a few times, kids in tow. I attempted to transition from a professional to a stay-at-home mom of two while my husband left the military to begin a civilian life and career amidst a global recession. My mother died, and then we moved again. Each event took a toll on my spirit, our coping skills, and the ability of my husband and I to work as a team to transcend life challenges. In time, my marriage imploded and my husband wanted a divorce.

By 32 years old, I was soaked in insecurity, victimhood, and contempt; unrecognizable from my former self. I felt unable to cope and uncertain of a path forward.

After my husband and I separated, I desperately sought my first full-time job in years. Higher income was needed for single parenthood. Little did I know that my life would take a permanent turn for the better when I was hired to run a new program at a high-end Malibu treatment center: a men-only drug and sex addiction recovery program. This was the first and only program of its kind, created by Dr. Rob Weiss, a man who changed the trajectory of both my personal and professional life (and aspects of addiction treatment) forever.

The program's development was revolutionary in the addiction recovery world because of its uniquely integrative approach to defining addiction. It recognized that many addicts tightly fuse their substance abuse patterns with compulsive sexual behaviors or toxic relationship cycles. Without this integrative approach where all unhealthy patterns were identified and redefined, such addicts often relapsed related to the untreated (usually sexual) part of their addiction. Dr. Weiss's program felt that individuals with paired/fused substance and sex/romance issues needed to be treated for both halves of their addiction simultaneously. Otherwise, lasting sobriety was unlikely. (Over the years, this approach has proven effective, especially with certain chronically relapsing substance abusers.)

Under Dr. Weiss's supervision, I was tasked with running this innovative treatment center, a job that both excited me and intimidated the hell out of me.

Realizing what a phenomenal opportunity this could be, I set out to meet this challenge the same way I'd dealt with every other challenge I'd ever faced: like a Type A control freak. I was going to out-perform and out-work all of my anxieties, doubts, and vulnerabilities. I was going to be the best damn paired substance/sex addiction program director in the world. Whatever that meant.

As occurs in many rehabs, the treatment curriculum was based heavily in teachings related to the 12-Steps, and clients were required to attend 12-Step meetings. We also assigned homework tasks based on the 12 steps.

I quickly learned that most of my colleagues were in 12-Step recovery programs themselves and, therefore, were well-versed in the lingo and application of the steps. They could quote parts of the "Big Book" of Alcoholics Anonymous, and they used all sorts of language that I had never heard before to describe addicts and their struggles. These sayings included wonderful little aphorisms like:

- The disease is trying to kill you.
- Tell the truth and tell it faster.
- First things first.
- One day at a time.
- Just do the next right thing.
- If nothing changes, nothing changes.

At first, I thought I *knew enough* about the 12 Steps because my previous jobs and education had glossed over them. "How complicated can this be?" I thought. "They're 12 sentences written on big posters that hang on the walls in recovery meetings and treatment centers, and they seem really straightforward." Plus, the 12 Step books appeared to be filled with easily understood personal accounts of alcoholics and addicts struggling to recover and heal. It all seemed easy enough to understand and implement. So I told myself, "I've got this. No problem."

In retrospect, I made the same naive mistake that many people make when they are first introduced to 12-Step concepts and material: over-simplifying and under-appreciating the magnitude of a time-tested, worldwide program that has helped millions of people (including countless non-addicts) change their lives for the better. To members of 12-Step fellowships, the steps are far more than a few sentences on a poster. The 12 Steps represent a community, an accountability structure, and a system of challenging and restructuring flawed ways of thinking and acting. Most of all, they are a proven pathway way out of one's own misery.

The 12 Steps represent a community, an accountability structure, and a system of challenging and restructuring flawed ways of thinking and acting.

Every day I spent with clients and running the treatment program, I became more intrigued by and in awe of Alcoholics Anonymous (AA) and other 12 Step programs (Narcotics Anonymous, Sex Addicts Anonymous, Sex and Love Addicts Anonymous, Gamblers Anonymous, Overeaters Anonymous, etc.). I was blown away when I realized how many misconceptions and misunderstandings that I and the general public held about addiction, recovery, and the 12 Steps; blown away to the point where I've devoted my career to changing this.

My intrigue peaked as I repeatedly witnessed the undeniable, life-altering impact the 12 Steps had on both my clients and my colleagues. I watched clients enter treatment broken and highly defensive, incredibly protective of the intensely harmful and destructive behaviors in which they routinely engaged. Then, after treatment and active engagement in the 12-Step community—exploring the material, applying it to their lives and stories—I saw them transform from monsters into men. They morphed from narcissistic, destructive, seeming sociopaths to vulnerable, empathetic, and compassionate humans. I had never witnessed such drastic transformations before.

Importantly, all of this was taking place at a time when I, too, was desperate for change and relief from pain and suffering.

I wondered, *How does this simple list of steps help people find relief from a devastating and mind-boggling disease like addiction? And if addicts are able to entirely transform their lives using this program, can a non-addict like myself also use these steps for positive change?* Driven by intrigue and desperation, I soaked up every book, every training session with Dr. Weiss, and every story shared by colleagues about their recovery. I learned concepts and tools I had never been taught in my years of education and training as a mental health therapist. Aside from enhancing my professional skills, the 12 Steps appealed to me as the most effective, constructive path forward from my personal crisis.

This book is a collection of everything I learned on my path toward growth and healing. A path that began nearly a decade ago as a clinician trying to keep addicts alive when, in retrospect, they were the ones saving my life. Though I never shared my clients' symptoms of substance abuse and high-risk sexual behaviors, I did share many of the same emotional and mental scars.

Like the addicts I was treating, I was deeply wounded, insecure, raw, filled with shame, and had minimal awareness or tools with which to navigate my journey toward healing and living a more fulfilling life. It felt like I was fighting an unknown enemy in the dark and lashing out at anything and everything in the process. Then, finally, when that became exhausting enough, I was able to "surrender" to the reality of my life and enter into the 12-Step process. With that, I was able to work toward a better understanding of myself and others. Eventually, I found that I could live a conscious, congruent, and empowered existence.

However, as with all growth, the journey is an infinite one. Life continues to be imperfect. I still struggle with certain issues like being controlling, judgmental, and passive-aggressive. Still, I would never choose to return to my previous, unconscious life before I discovered and began to practice the 12 Steps. Retrospectively, I see all that the 12 Steps have given me: more intimate and fulfilling relationships, shame resiliency, less self-righteousness, and more honesty. I have clarity in who I am and who I want around me. I also credit this work with improving my capacity for empathy, compassion, and forgiveness—all skills that helped my husband and I eventually work toward healing our marriage and family.

While there were many influences and events that have collectively contributed to my healing and growth, I credit the 12 Steps (and those who taught them to me) with igniting the change process and pushing me forward in a safe, structured way. Not identifying as an addict did not preclude me from engaging with the 12-Step community, nor did it stop me from finding applicable stories and concepts. Finding the commonalities (rather than focusing on the differences) I had with addicts allowed me to enter into a process of lasting growth that profoundly altered the way I live, love, think, and behave. The 12 Steps presented a safe, structured, approachable, and proven way for me to challenge my former way of thinking and living—a way to shift into an entirely different system of life.

Not identifying as an addict did not preclude me from engaging with the 12-Step community, nor did it stop me from finding applicable stories and concepts.

An Addict (Scott) Finds the 12 Steps

Unlike Kristin, I came to the 12 Steps as an active addict—alcohol, drugs, and sex. I was an absolute mess. My career was in shambles, my family was aghast, and hardly anyone I knew was even talking to me.

I thought I'd been doing such a great job of covering things up. But apparently people noticed when I didn't show up for work, when I made plans to hang out and then canceled at the last minute pretending to be sick, and when they occasionally got calls from me in the middle of the night asking them to bail me out of jail. I thought that if I was still employed (however tenuously) and still paying the bills, then everything must be OK, right?

But my life was anything but OK. I was hitting rock bottom and the people around me were not happy about it. One of them suggested I might have an issue with addiction. Then someone else said the same thing. Then my work suggested that perhaps I would benefit from treatment. Then my lawyer said the same thing. It was the lawyer's suggestion that did it. Maybe because I grew up with a lawyer father; more likely because I was tired of waking up in rooms where the door locked on the outside rather than the inside.

So finally, about 20 years past due, I sought help from an addiction therapist. But let me be clear here: I didn't come into addiction recovery so I could heal or change my behaviors. I came into recovery because I wanted the consequences I was experiencing to go away, and because I thought that someone might tell me who I should blame for all the problems in my life. I did not see that I had a part in the disaster my life had become.

Even when I finally went to see a therapist for help, I resisted. I kept secrets about the full extent of my problems, I said I would take my therapist's advice but didn't (and then I would lie to him about it), and I only went to a 12-Step meeting when he very politely but firmly told me that if I didn't, he would have to fire me as a client.

I've now been in recovery for slightly more than 20 years, and the longer I've been around, the more I've come to understand that I was incredibly unhappy in my addiction. I was lonely. I was bored. My life had become very, very small. There was work. There was addiction. And that was it.

As obvious as it may have been to others that the consequences I was facing were my own fault, I was not able to accept and process that idea for quite some time. Instead of taking responsibility, I blamed my parents. Then I blamed society. And religion. And the internet. I blamed any person or institution that either directly or indirectly impacted my life, telling myself they were the cause of my addictive behaviors and therefore my problems.

I pointed the finger at absolutely everyone but the person who was staring back at me in the mirror.

Sure, I knew that if *someone else* was behaving the way I was behaving, that person would obviously have a problem that he or she needed to deal with. But not me. I was different because.... And then I would fill in the blank with any idea that popped into my head, no matter how crazy.

I justified my addiction with stories like:

- My mother was too close to me and that messed me up.
- I was probably molested (even though I had no memory of that).
- My parents never accepted me for who I am.
- Our society is sexually repressed. In Europe, they're much freer about sex.
- Everyone I know drinks and gets high. So that can't be my problem.

My list of rationalizations was lengthy, and nothing on that list ever had anything at all to do with me making a conscious choice to behave in a certain way. Even when my life spiraled out of control and I finally entered therapy and 12-Step recovery, I did not see that my choices were *mine*. In fact, I spent most of my first year of treatment blaming others, especially my parents (who, in reality, are lovely people), for my problems.

Finally, one day in a 12-Step meeting, at a time when I felt that I had mellowed a bit about my parents' perceived role in creating my addiction, I said, "I suppose my mom and dad would have been really good parents for a different kid, but they didn't get *me* or properly support *me*." And I truly felt that statement was a generous and kind interpretation of my childhood.

Then an old-timer sitting next to me snorted and said, "You're probably not what they had in mind, either." Everyone in the room laughed (except for me) because it was a really funny comment. And then, after the meeting, the old-timer pulled me aside to say, "I meant what I said, you know." Then he suggested that maybe it was time for me to start working the 12 Steps instead of just paying lip-service to "making big changes" in my life.

That was the moment I began to look at myself as *maybe* having some responsibility for my addiction and my life.

No, I did not immediately figure out that the mess my life had become was entirely and completely my fault. But I did slowly begin to understand and accept that although my addictions may have started as a coping mechanism for dealing with unresolved childhood issues, nobody ever held a gun to my head and said, "Engage in your addiction or else." I also came to understand and accept that even after I knew that my addictive behaviors were out of control and creating significant problems in my life, I chose to continue with those behaviors. So, when my life fell apart, it was nobody's fault but my own.

Today, I am grateful for that old-timer's comment. It was a much-needed spark for embarking on my 12-Step journey—a journey that has slowly but steadily changed how I think about my behaviors, my life, and my connections to the people around me.

I'm also happy to say that after many conversations with that old-timer (now a close friend), along with a considerable amount of therapy, working the 12 Steps (especially Step 4), and sitting in on literally thousands of recovery meetings, I understand that my addiction is my own. Yes, there may be issues that underlie my addiction that are not of my doing, but the choice to engage in addictive behaviors can only be made by me.

Today, slightly more than 20 years into my process of recovery and healing, I have two mentors that I'm privileged to work with and interact with on an almost daily basis, Dr. Robert Weiss (also a mentor of Kristin's) and Dr. David Fawcett. And both men, well-known and highly respected pillars of the recovery community, preach one thing above all else: the need to feel intimately connected.

The longer I am sober, the better I understand this maxim.

My active addiction was a 20-plus year effort to push away feelings of disconnection and loneliness. I was desperate for intimate connection, but rather than becoming vulnerable and reaching out to others in ways that would let them know the real me, I built an emotional wall that kept them away. I did and said a thousand different things each and every day that told the people around me, "I don't need you or want you, so please don't invade my space."

I did this because I was afraid. I thought that if I became vulnerable, if I showed you my true self, you would think I was weak, or needy, or defective, or just plain unworthy. I thought you would reject me, laugh at me, leave me stranded and alone forever. So I beat you to the punch, pulling away and walling myself off so I would never have to feel that pain.

And yes, I see the irony (now) in longing for intimate connection but never taking the risks that must be taken to build it.

I was lonely and miserable. I didn't know that, of course, because I never let myself feel it. Instead, I numbed myself with addictive substances and behaviors. That's what addicts do, right? When we feel emotional discomfort, we escape it by any means necessary, even when our addictions and our isolation are killing us—body and soul alike.

I thank my Higher Power every day that my world finally collapsed, that I finally hit bottom, that I finally realized that I couldn't live the way I was living any longer because I wasn't actually living. I was avoiding life. I was a walking zombie. By fearing and avoiding intimate connection, I was missing out on the things that make life worthwhile. I wasn't feeling any pain, but I wasn't feeling any joy, either. In an effort to stay safe, I'd made choices that kept me "apart from" despite the fact that what I truly wanted and needed was to be "a part of." And sadly, that state of being was an inside job. My loneliness and misery were *my* loneliness and misery. The people around me were not the problem; I was the problem.

In an effort to stay safe, I'd made choices that kept me "apart from" despite the fact that what I truly wanted and needed was to be "a part of."

That is a lesson I learned as I worked the 12 Steps. It's not a lesson I wanted or expected to learn. What I wanted from 12-Step recovery was for people to think I was addressing my issues so I could keep my job, stay out of jail, not lose my home, keep talking to my family, etc. I was not interested in meaningful change; I wanted my consequences to stop, and that's about it. But 12-Step recovery has a way of sinking in and healing us whether we want it to or not.

In 12-Step meetings, my fellow addicts continually greeted me with smiles and hugs. They continually asked how I was doing and then listened when I answered. Then they said things like, "We're going for coffee after the meeting. Will you join us?" and, "We'll see you tomorrow, right?" They even wheedled my phone number out of me, and they actually picked up the phone and called me.

In the early stages of recovery, I could barely tolerate these efforts to connect. Hugs made me want to jump out of my skin. I was terrified of a ringing phone. And talking (and laughing!) over coffee with a group of people? No way could I manage that. But I also knew, on some deep level, that these loving individuals were offering me the empathetic, nonjudgmental, emotionally intimate connection that I'd craved my entire life. They were also offering guidance, through the 12 Steps, on how I could let go of my shame, work on my character shortcomings, and learn to relate in healthier ways.

Eventually, I started to look forward to these genial overtures and the accompanying advice I received, and then I started, slowly, to make the changes I needed to make. Now, many years later, these wonderful men and women are integral *and emotionally intimate* parts of my daily life. They know me, even the parts of me that I'd rather conceal, and they love me anyway. Unconditionally. I know them, too, and love them in the same way. I am no longer lonely and miserable. I no longer push people away. Instead, I take emotional risks because the 12 Steps have taught me the joy of being known and accepted and cared for as the person I truly am.

Why This Book Was Written (Kristin)

As occurs in the 12-Step recovery community, Scott and I are hoping to share our stories with you in hopes that our strengths and struggles may help you identify, understand, and catalyze your own path toward change. Often, hearing another's story of struggle and healing can bring clarity to our own problems and potential solutions.

Looking back on my own story, I can barely believe how little I understood about myself and what I was going through. It took hearing other's (mostly the addicts I was working with and occasionally my recovering addict co-workers) candidly honest accounts of their own shame, embarrassment, and mistakes to shake me from my trance of complacency. Their courage to own and share their stories gave me the courage to own and share mine.

But plenty (probably most) non-addicts think that the 12 Steps can only be used by addicts. That is not the case. And that is why we have written this book. We want to help the countless thousands of non-addicted but still struggling people we've encountered in treatment centers, private practice, online communities, and other outlets. Even though these individuals may not identify as addicts, they are in deep struggle due to mental health issues, shame, betrayal, trauma, or other unhealthy relationship dynamics that they find too confusing to name or explain.

By the end of the book, we hope that non-addict readers (and also addicts who choose to read this book) will have a clearer understanding of the things we do as humans that contribute to our unhappiness and sense of devastation. Using the 12 Steps as guideposts, we will provide helpful tools and coaching toward a path out of the cycle of insanity and dysfunction. This book will also be useful to loved ones of addicts who aren't necessarily struggling themselves but would like to better understand addiction and the 12-Step recovery process.

Basically, this book is for anyone who wants to get out of a painful internal or interpersonal cycle and seek a better way of living.

You don't need to be an addict and you don't need extreme or obvious symptoms such as debilitating depression or anxiety to get something meaningful from this book. You don't even need to be in relationship with an addict. The simple truth is that people in deep struggle can appear to be quite high functioning. I know I was adept at putting on a good show while lying to myself and others about how badly I was drowning. In fact, I feel like many of those who *appear* to need this book the least may benefit the most.

As you begin this journey with us, remember that it wasn't without uncomfortable, humbling work, extreme setbacks, tons of errors, and ever-present re-dos that Scott and I were able to change for the better. But the change happened. And not just with us as individuals, but our entire family systems and friendships. And it's *still* happening. The journey keeps revealing more work for us to do, more progress to make. Luckily for us, the 12 Steps are as applicable and useful today as on day one.

For these and many other reasons, we believe the 12 Steps should be explored by every person looking to move to that higher frequency in life—addicted or not. We also believe (in fact, we *know* from experience) that any 12-Step journey is fraught with challenges and adversity. But these journeys are nonetheless invaluable, as they help those who are willing to work toward a pathway to enlightenment, self-esteem, and empowered living.

How This Book Came About (Scott)

About ten years ago, I started writing full-time, something I'd always wanted to do but that never seemed possible in active addiction or even in early recovery, when I was mostly trying to just make it through the day. Initially, I wanted to write fiction. Novels and films. And I did do a bit of that. But I found that I preferred to write about things that are inherently meaningful to me and a significant portion of the people I interact with on a daily basis: addiction, mental health, and the process of healing. So I decided to do exactly that, and I've never looked back.

Over the years, I've ghostwritten or otherwise contributed to more than 20 books focused on addiction, mental health, and recovery, along with numerous scholarly articles, popular press articles, and blogs. Today, I work as the Director of Content Development for a company called Seeking Integrity. We have a sex, porn, and paired substance/sex addiction treatment center in Los Angeles, and an extensive free resource website (SexandRelationshipHealing.com) for addicts, loved ones of addicts, and professionals.

As part of my work with Seeking Integrity, I wrote a series of articles on how addicts can best work the 12 Steps, and why they should do so. At approximately the same time, Kristin was writing a series of articles for SexandRelationshipHealing.com about how non-addicts can benefit from working the 12 Steps. At that point, coming together to create a book seemed like fate. And who were we to argue with Mother Kismet?

So here we are.

As you can likely tell already, Kristin and I are big believers in the power of the 12 Steps, as first developed by Alcoholics Anonymous (AA) and later adapted for use by other 12-Step recovery programs. Mostly we believe in the power of the steps because we've worked the steps, and we've helped others work the steps, and we know what a life-changing experience this can be.

That said, working the 12 Steps can seem a bit daunting. Sure, when you first read the steps, they seem relatively logical and straightforward. They probably even make sense. But when you think about actually doing them, about turning your life over to a Higher Power, about dredging up your worst moments and talking about them with another person, about making amends for your wrongs to people you're still incredibly angry with.... Yeah, right. That's not going to happen. No way, no how, forget about it.

Well, guess what? Working the 12 Steps, doing all those things that sound incredibly awful to you when you first learn about them, is a precious and undeniable path to healing and living a happier, more rewarding life. Working with a therapist is typically the beginning of this process, and for a lot of people it is an essential part of the process. But changing your life for the better over the long-haul, establishing meaningful connections, and finding serenity and happiness requires ongoing work, and a significant part of that work can be done by practicing the 12 Steps.

Our Caveat

This brief guidebook is an effort to demystify the 12 Steps, primarily for non-addicts but also for addicts who may read this book. Hopefully, we can take away or at least diminish your fear of working them.

That said, the information we present is *not the only way* to work the 12 Steps, and we won't even try to pretend that it is. In fact, there are as many ways to work the 12 Steps as there are people working them. Rather than telling you that we're presenting *the way* to work the steps, or even *our way* to work the steps, we will simply restate the advice that we've heard over and over both in and out of 12-Step meetings: *Take what you like and leave the rest.* If the material presented makes sense to you, then use it. And if it doesn't make sense to you, that does not in any way mean that the 12 Steps are flawed; it just means this guidebook isn't the best pathway for you.

Ultimately, the methodology you decide to use when working the 12 Steps is not important. What's important is that you work the steps, because, as stated above, ongoing step-work is a proven route to better living. So please go to meetings appropriate to your issue, please get a sponsor, please build a support group, and please talk with others about their experience working the steps. Each and every one of these individuals will have something useful to offer you, and before you know it, you'll be helping them, too. You will be as important to these folks and their recovery as they are to you and yours.

No matter what, we encourage all loved ones of addicts to find support. Addicts are incredibly complicated and can be unbelievably difficult to love and care for—no matter how hard you try. Moreover, loved ones of addicts are often labeled as codependent, which tends to feel shaming and blaming, as if they are somehow at fault for the addict's shortcomings. We prefer the term "prodependent" and recommend reading Dr. Rob Weiss's book,

Prodependence, which was written to change how therapists and people in general think about and work with caregiving loved ones. If the new 12-Step group Prodependence Anonymous has meetings in your area, you may want to check that out.

As for reading and utilizing this book, you might want to read it cover-to-cover and then go back and start applying the 12 Steps in your life, perhaps working with a 12-Step sponsor or an addiction therapist who fully understands the steps and how to work them. You might also want to read just one step at a time, first seeing how and why addicts do a particular step (as explained by Scott); then learning how you, as a non-addict, might implement and benefit from that same step (as explained by Kristin). No matter what, please read both sections—addicts and non-addicts—as they offer complementary insight. And please do the exercises at the end of each chapter, as they will help you incorporate your experience into the 12 Steps.

However it is that you decide to approach reading—all at once or one step at a time—working the steps is likely to be more effective if you do so with guidance from a knowledgeable person, preferably someone who has worked the steps themselves. As part of this work, we encourage you to do the exercises we present at the end of each chapter. We have done those exercises ourselves and found them beneficial, and we have led others through the same process with similar results.

Some of the early readers of our working manuscript posed an interesting question: How do I know when I'm done with one step and ready to move on to the next step. The easy answer to this question is that your therapist or sponsor (or whoever else it is that's guiding you through your 12-Step work) will usually say, "OK, that's good for now. Let's move on to the next task." The more difficult answer is that you are never done with any of the steps. The 12 Steps are a lifelong process of learning. Almost every person who fully works the steps finds themselves revisiting certain steps on an as-needed basis. But generally, if you've done the exercises we suggest in this book and you feel like you've gained an understanding of yourself and your life, and your 12-Step mentor agrees with that, then you're probably ready to move forward with the next step.

At all times, please understand that this book is not the be-all, end-all when it comes to understanding and practicing the 12 Steps. Far from it, in fact. If your sponsor or therapist has other insight and suggestions, do not discount their input simply because it doesn't match the advice that we offer in these pages. Countless people know as much about the steps as we do; a lot of them probably know more. Perhaps a lot more. We accept that, we're 100 percent cool with it, and we're 100 percent open to learning from those incredible individuals. We hope that you will be, too.

Lastly, before sending you on your journey, we believe it is important to warn you that at various points in this guidebook we use the word "God" or the words "Higher Power." Please don't be turned off by this. We do not espouse a specific religion or deity, nor does any 12-Step program. When you see the words "God" and "Higher Power," feel free to substitute any term that you are comfortable with, because religious belief is not a requirement for healing.

One final note: 12-Step recovery is a journey. It is meant to be enjoyed, so take your time and revel in each tiny success. You don't have to "be well" by tomorrow. In fact, you don't ever have to be well. The true goal of 12-Step recovery is to do life better today than yesterday.

Enjoy your journey!

Addict or Non-Addict: What's the Difference?

Before you pass judgment on someone who's self-destructing, it's important to remember they usually aren't trying to destroy themselves. They're trying to destroy something inside that doesn't belong.
—James Storm

At first, addiction is maintained by pleasure, but the intensity of this pleasure gradually diminishes and the addiction is then maintained by the avoidance of pain.
—Frank Tallis

Understanding Addiction

Despite addiction killing tens of thousands of Americans each year and negatively impacting millions more, there are widespread misconceptions about addiction—its causes, symptoms, and the path to recovery. There is significant evidence that 12-Step recovery is one of the most effective paths to helping addicts not only survive but thrive, despite their lifelong disease. Yet despite the many obviously redeeming qualities, the 12 Steps and related tools of recovery remain a mystery to most, especially to those who are not themselves addicted.

We are baffled that the 12 Steps aren't as mainstream as "The Golden Rule" or any other guiding principle or theological construct. Even the non-religious can recite at least a few of the Ten Commandments and understand that basic moral code. But how many people know even one of the 12 Steps?

We believe the continued resistance to examining the 12-Step model lies in its strong correlation with the addiction field and our culture's negative stigma and misunderstanding of addiction. Therefore, we feel like we need to take a moment to help you understand some important basics about addiction so you can see how relatable and common addictive tendencies are to *everyone.* In other words, we want you to understand that non-addicts and addicts are more alike than different.

First and foremost, people are erroneous in thinking addiction is about the substance or the addictive behavior engaged in by the addict. Ultimately, addictions are not about feeling good and having a good time, they're about feeling less and avoiding emotional discomfort. Addicts drink, get high, and engage in addictive behaviors to "numb out" and escape from stress and emotional discomfort, including the pain of underlying emotional and psychological issues like depression, anxiety, loneliness, boredom, unresolved early-life trauma, and the like. Whatever the addiction, addicts are not seeking fun and pleasure; they are trying to control and manage their feelings by "escaping" into an addiction.

Ultimately, addictions are not about feeling good and having a good time, they're about feeling less and avoiding emotional discomfort.

Unfortunately for addicts, the escape they get is temporary. When they are done acting in their addiction (when they "sober up"), whatever it is that they were trying to not feel is still there, often laced with feelings of guilt and shame about the addictive behavior in which they just engaged. So, what do addicts do? They go right back to self-medicating their feelings with alcohol, drugs, cigarettes, food, sex, porn, gambling, spending, or whatever else it is that they use for distraction and emotional escape.

Addicts are not alone in this tendency to numb their feelings. Non-addicts do this as well. When non-addicts feel overwhelmed, they turn to their own escapist coping mechanisms. If they're exceptionally emotionally and psychologically healthy, they will easily and automatically reach out to empathetic loved ones to share what they're experiencing so they can feel validated, understood, and maybe even ask for advice about how to proceed. If they're less emotionally and psychologically healthy, they may take the healthy route and reach out for support, or they might lash out in anger, attempt to control the behavior of others, run away, or just shut down, unable to function at all.

In this respect, non-addicts are not so different from addicts. When faced with stress and other forms of emotional discomfort, both groups cope, at least some of the time, in maladaptive ways. Usually, addicted or not, we turn to unhealthy coping mechanisms because unresolved early-life trauma (abuse, neglect, inconsistent parenting, and the like) have poisoned the well of interpersonal attachment. In other words, we have learned, usually very early in life, that caregiving loved ones will not always be there for us in the ways we might hope, so rather than automatically turning to those individuals when we're struggling, we will sometimes (or habitually) turn to a substance or an escapist behavior. Who among us hasn't had a bad day and gone for a pint of Ben & Jerry's or a video game or a trashy TV show instead of asking for help?

In his book, *In the Realm of Hungry Ghosts*, Gabor Maté writes: "A hurt is at the center of all addictive behaviors." We believe that this is true, and that it applies equally to non-addicts when they are struggling in some way. Basically, thanks to unresolved early-life trauma, we associate fear rather than comfort with human intimacy and attachment. Thus, we refuse to turn to others, even loved ones, for help when we're struggling or feeling down. Instead, if we're addicted, we compulsively and obsessively self-soothe by numbing out with an addictive substance or behavior. And if we're not addicted, we stuff our feelings, we people-please, we rage, we micro-manage, we.... Well, you get the idea. Like addicts, non-addicts can use unhealthy coping skills to manage their mental health, stability, emotional pain, and shame.

"Normies" (non-addicts) like to think that addicts are some separate species of humans. Often, normies can't wrap their brain around how someone would drink themselves into oblivion or use drugs until they've lost everything. The irony is that those same people will observe addicts' behaviors, scratching their heads in disbelief, while checking their phones for the hundredth time that day, eating chocolate cake the doctor has implored them to avoid because they're pre-diabetic, online shopping themselves into impossible debt, and raging at family members they supposedly hold precious.

We all do things that seem crazy and unhealthy at various seasons of our lives. We all face challenges with varying levels of intensity. The difference between addicts and non-addicts is simply a matter of how we choose to cope. Do we reach out in healthy ways, do we turn to an addiction, or do we turn to some other maladaptive behavior?

If our attempts to cope are in any way maladaptive, the 12 Steps can help. In working the 12 Steps, we identify the problems in our lives, we examine our role in those problems, and then we make changes to better not only ourselves but our relationships. Because healthy relationships are what it's all about. When we develop healthier relationships with ourselves and those around us, we no longer feel a need to turn to the unhealthy coping mechanisms we've relied upon for so many years to make it through the day.

In working the 12 Steps, we identify the problems in our lives, we examine our role in those problems, and then we make changes to better not only ourselves but our relationships. Because healthy relationships are what it's all about.

This is as true for non-addicts as addicts.

We all have pain and distress. We all hurt. We're all afraid. We all do what we can to cope. And sometimes our attempts to cope do more harm than good. That's the human condition. Sure, it's possible there are a few unicorns out there with perfect coping skills all the time in every situation, but we doubt it. If those people do exist, we've not met them. Nor do we expect to.

Russell Brand, a British actor who's been outspoken about his use of the 12 Steps to recover from drug abuse and sex addiction, explains that we are all working some kind of "program" as we live our daily lives. These programs may be a 12-Step program, a religious construct, a set of cultural filters and biases, or behaviors and choices based on our childhood wounds. Whatever they are, they are programs we use to live our lives.

Similarly, in *Breathing Under Water*, Richard Rohr asserts that we are all addicts, in theory. He writes, "Human beings are addictive by nature.... We're addicted to our own habitual way of doing anything, our own defenses, and most especially, our patterned way of thinking, or how we process reality." Rohr then states that people who struggle with substance abuse or a behavioral addiction only display the most visible of addictions. Other people find ways to creatively disguise their addictions with cultural norms—leading them into unhealthy relationships, issues with food or money, obsessions with performance or appearance, etc.

These "addicts in disguise" live under the radar, so to speak. They aren't struggling with an obvious addiction, or obviously abusive relationships, or obviously deep depression or anxiety. In fact, their lives may look fine on the surface. However, similar to addicts, they continually turn to external sources as they try to fill a void that can only be filled internally.

In retrospect, we both (one addict, one non-addict) realize that we were completely blind to the fact that we, too, lived in our individual patterns of "isms" and behaviors. The false and counterproductive beliefs that drove our lives were imbued in us by our upbringings and environments, and they kept us in an unhappy state. It is only with a greater perspective, many years into 12-Step healing, that we realize our former belief systems and false programs for fulfillment and happiness were making us miserable.

Addict or not, we all seek external sources to validate us, to help us escape from discomfort and pain, and to help us feel like we're good enough. The problem is that these external sources of value, worth, and intensity are fleeting. They are false shelters from the storm of shame that constantly whispers, "Are you sure you're good enough? Are you sure you're worthy of love and belonging?"

Worse still, when any of our go-to external coping skills are removed (i.e., our relationship ends, our looks fade, the money is gone, the drugs don't work anymore, etc.), we find ourselves exposed to the full force and harshness of our lives. Our reality surfaces, and we find ourselves drowning in shame and other forms of emotional pain.

Many of us, whether we are addicted or not, then manifest the addict's definition of insanity: doing the same thing over and over but expecting different results. We do this with diet, jobs, parenting, relationships, money, and every other aspect of life. We engage in the same defense mechanisms we've always used to feel good enough, to survive, and to make it through the day, even though these mechanisms are not working anymore.

Ironically, the counterintuitive answer to this insanity is buried in the layers of the 12 Steps:

- Own that things aren't working for you anymore.
- Realize you can't do this alone because your best thinking got you here.
- Surrender to a Higher Power.
- Do some serious personality analysis and shame resilience work.
- Connect with others and reconnect with yourself.
- Be accountable for your choices and make amends for your transgressions.
- Continue to pursue personal growth and be of service to others.

After working and studying the 12 Steps, we both believe that we are supposed to be imperfect. Our Higher Power created us to be flawed and make mistakes. Our Higher Power did this so we can learn from our missteps. Our Higher Power understands that when we own and accept our shortcomings, harms, and pain, it creates a deeper level of complexity and compassion within us, and we grow from the humility this creates.

The more we're invested in escape, the more shame-filled and miserable we are. It is only when we see and accept our mistakes and shortcomings that we grow and prosper. This means we need to feel and work through our shame and pain to grow as people. And, in our opinion, this is true for *everyone*. So non-addicts can find as much transformation and enlightenment in the 12 Steps as addicts do. The 12 Steps, for every person, are timeless concepts that are worth exploring and pondering at any phase of life.

We hope that all of you non-addicts (and also the addicts) will join us on this journey with an open heart and mind.

The following is a short quiz to help you identify areas of your life where you may currently be struggling and seeking improvement.

1. Do you find yourself regularly comparing parts of yourself, your life, your relationships, or your achievements with others?
2. Do you regularly find yourself saying "yes" to someone's request when you would much rather say no (but you don't want to disappoint them or make them mad)?
3. Do you find that you become angry or extremely bothered when you think others are upset at you?
4. Do you require approval from others to feel good about yourself?
5. Do you act nice to others on the outside but really feel like "I can't stand you" or "I'm so angry with you" on the inside?
6. Do you often remain silent to keep the peace? Do you say things like "I'll be the bigger person" or "I'm sure things will get better after (fill in the blank)" but continue to feel angry, hurt, and frustrated?
7. Do you believe that if you make mistakes you have failed? Do you feel embarrassed by your mistakes (and maybe try to hide them from others)? Are you fearful of taking risks?
8. Do you find yourself criticizing others to feel better about yourself?
9. Do you struggle with complimenting or affirming others in your life?
10. Do you lie or omit the truth to avoid conflict or because "what they don't know isn't going to hurt them"?

11. Do you find yourself avoiding looking weak or foolish to others for not having the answer? Do you sometimes just lie or make up an answer?
12. Do you have to be doing something exceptional to feel alive or passionate? Do you find yourself feeling bored and exploring ways to escape the monotony of life?
13. Do you find yourself avoiding phone calls or isolating from others to avoid a person or an uncomfortable situation?
14. Do you have to be needed by someone to feel alive and useful?
15. Do you often feel resentful because someone needs you too much?
16. Do you regularly find yourself feeling disappointed by others and feel like you're the only person you can count on to meet your needs?
17. Do you find yourself doing things you *think* others will want you to do to please them or to stop them from getting mad at you?
18. Do you find yourself bragging or showing off your assets or achievements to cover up feelings of inadequacy or uncertainty?
19. Do you find yourself negatively judging people's choices or behaviors, or their children's choices or behaviors?
20. When others are happy with you, are you happy? When others are unhappy with you, are you unhappy?

If you answered yes to any of these questions, you could benefit from exploring yourself and your relationships further through the 12-Step journey.

Why Addicts and Non-Addicts Sometimes Approach the 12 Steps Differently

Addiction treatment specialists sometimes use the diagnosis of diabetes type II as a metaphor to explain addiction and its treatment. Like addiction, diabetes is an affliction that millions suffer from. That said, the severity of each case varies, along with the amount of intervention needed. Most importantly, the best treatments in the world can't save those who aren't willing to dramatically alter their entire lifestyle (eating habits, sleep, physical activity, stress management, etc.) The same is true for addicts.

A diabetic seeking guidance and assistance in changing his or her lifestyle will go about changes differently than someone who simply wants to lose 20 pounds. The main reason for this is the individual's motivation. For a non-diabetic, it's important to make healthy food choices and remain active to stay healthy. For a diabetic, making healthy food choices and exercising regularly can be the difference between life and death.

The same basic dichotomy appears with non-addicts and addicts. Non-addicts may feel unhappy, discontented, and stuck in unhealthy, undesirable patterns. Addicts, however, are watching their relationships, finances, health, and lives disintegrate in front of their very eyes. For non-addicts, the 12 Steps can lead to a healthier, happier, more connected life. For addicts, the 12 Steps are life and death. There is an intrinsic difference in motivation.

Non-addicts may slip in and out of seasons of struggle, so they can take it or leave it with recovery and healing. For addicts, no matter the season or struggle, they simply cannot return to their old addictive patterns. For them, the old patterns are all-consuming and incredibly destructive, sometimes even deadly.

To Abstain or Not to Abstain

Alcoholics Anonymous (the original source of 12 Steps) welcomes anyone who has a desire to stop drinking. AA celebrates and honors all participants' sobriety dates—the day they stopped using alcohol. Abstinence (versus harm-reduction) is a core tenet of most 12-Step programs. For non-addicts, however, abstinence may be a more obscure concept to adopt or follow. In lieu of focusing on a substance, non-addicts should focus on dysfunctional behaviors that consistently create problems for them.

Thus, the 12-Step journey for non-addicts is focused on becoming more aware of behaviors, patterns, and people that are no longer working in their life. This means non-addicts do not have to narrowly define what must be ceased and terminated, as addicts do. For non-addicts, the 12 Steps are an invitation to explore their lives and see what comes up for them.

Sometimes—not always—it is determined that the healthiest path for a non-addict is to fully and permanently abstain from certain behaviors and unhealthy relationship patterns. Other times, they simply need to take a break from such things, using the "time off" to develop clarity on important concepts, such as the underlying thoughts and feelings that drive the problem behavior, the power that behavior has over them, and what that behavior may be covering up or causing them to avoid.

Not Addicted, But...

Sam sought therapy after a long pattern of staying in relationships with women he didn't feel strongly connected to. He described beginning a relationship feeling deeply for each woman but suddenly, and without full understanding, wanting to push them away and end the relationship. Once the women tired of trying to emotionally re-engage him, they would also pull away and eventually they would break up with him. That would trigger Sam to chase after them and want to get back into a relationship with them. Then the cycle would continue.

Sam reported that many of the women would tell him he was emotionally unavailable. He found there was always a constant push and pull in the relationship. He felt they would use him, and he would happily, at first, take on the role of caretaker and "savior" to these women, thinking it was love. But then he would feel smothered and pull away. They would engage in months of back and forth—breaking up and getting back together—until one of them would cut ties permanently and move on with someone else.

After years of chaos and confusion, Sam decided to temporarily abstain from all romantic relationships while he reassessed his life. During this period of abstinence, he attended therapy, re-engaged friend groups, and participated in creative outlets he'd formerly abandoned.

Sam's season of deep personal growth helped him realize that "being alone" and "not taking care of someone" weren't bad things to be avoided at all costs. He also realized that he struggled with valuing himself, that he was a womanizer, and that he had childhood trauma surrounding his early relationships. Many of these issues were masked by his pattern of trying to seduce and "take care of" women. He hadn't realized until then that he was avoiding an authentic, vulnerable, intimate relationship with an equal partner.

Realizations like Sam's are why abstinence from troubling behaviors, at least temporarily, is encouraged even for non-addicts.

The 12 Steps

1. We admitted we were powerless over alcohol [or drugs, sex, gambling, eating, shopping, etc.]—that our lives had become unmanageable.
2. Came to believe that a power greater than ourselves could restore us to sanity.
3. Made a decision to turn our will and our lives over to the care of God *as we understood God*.
4. Made a searching and fearless moral inventory of ourselves.
5. Admitted to God, to ourselves, and to another human being the exact nature of our wrongs.
6. Were entirely ready to have God remove all these defects of character.
7. Humbly asked God to remove our shortcomings.
8. Made a list of all persons we had harmed and became willing to make amends to them all.
9. Made direct amends to such people whenever possible, except when to do so would injure them or others.
10. Continued to take personal inventory, and when we were wrong promptly admitted it.
11. Sought through prayer and meditation to improve our conscious contact with God *as we understood God*, praying only for knowledge of God's will for us and the power to carry that out.

12. Having had a spiritual awakening as the result of these steps, we tried to carry this message to other alcoholics [or addicts], and to practice these principles in all our affairs.

Step 1 for Addicts

We admitted we were powerless over alcohol [or drugs, sex, gambling, eating, shopping, etc.]—that our lives had become unmanageable.

For a lot of addicts, walking into a treatment center, a therapist's office, or a 12-Step meeting for the first time is equivalent to working Step 1. The humble act of asking for help is, in and of itself, an admission of powerlessness and unmanageability. However, there is much more that an addict can and should do to fully work Step 1. Most of this work is designed to unearth the addict's complete history of addictive behaviors—the totality of the addiction and its consequences.

Task One: Consequences Inventory

For many addicts, addiction builds slowly over time, making it difficult to see how their lives have changed. Consequences that a casual outside observer could readily identify as severe can gradually become the norm. Thus, the insanity of addiction may look perfectly normal to the addict. The easiest way to break through this fog is to create a list of consequences related to addictive behaviors.

When addicts write out their consequences inventory, they are encouraged to list as many consequences as possible, breaking their list into the following categories:

- **Emotional Consequences:** These may include hopelessness, despair, guilt, shame, remorse, depression, paranoia, anxiety, loss of self-esteem, loneliness, emotional exhaustion, fear of going insane, feeling like two people (living a double-life), suicidal thoughts, homicidal thoughts, fear of the future, and more.
- **Physical Consequences:** These may include ulcers, high blood pressure, weight loss, weight gain, self-abuse (cutting, burning, etc.), unintentional injuries (falls, car wrecks, etc.), abuse by others, abuse to others, trouble sleeping or waking up, physical exhaustion, sexually transmitted diseases, attempted suicide, and more.
- **Spiritual Consequences:** These may include feeling disconnected, feeling abandoned, feeling anger toward a Higher Power, feelings of emptiness, loss of faith, loss of (or violation of) values and morals, loss of interest in the well-being of self and others, and more.
- **Family and Partnership Consequences:** These may include relationship strife, loss of respect, alienation, being disowned, threatened or actual loss of a spouse or partner, threatened or actual loss of parental rights, jeopardizing the family's well-being, and more.
- **Career and Educational Consequences:** These may include decreased performance, demotion, underemployment, loss of respect, poor grades or job reviews, not getting promoted, getting fired from a job or dismissed from school, losing a chance to work in one's career of choice, and more.
- **Other Consequences:** These may include loss of interest in formerly enjoyable activities, lack of self-care, loss of important friendships, loss of community standing, financial problems, involvement in illegal activities, near arrests, arrests, legal issues, incarceration, and more.

In my own addiction, I was completely disconnected from the

world, both physically and emotionally. At the time, I was living in Los Angeles, three blocks from my lifelong best friend and 45 minutes away from my sister in Orange County. Near the end of each week, my sister would call to see if I wanted to hang out with her and her kids. I would politely decline and tell her I had plans with my friend. Then my friend would call, and I would tell him I had plans with my sister. Then I would spend the weekend alone—drinking, drugging, and chasing sex.

Each night, I passed out rather than falling asleep. My diet consisted entirely of fast food and take-out from the Chinese restaurant across the street. My shins were perpetually covered in bruises from walking into my coffee table in a drunken stupor. My apartment was filthy. I was successful at my job at a small publishing house, but I had a reputation for being a bulldog—incredibly stubborn and prone to flashes of deep anger.

Any outside observer, if allowed to view the entirety of my life, could have easily spotted a major issue with addiction, but I could not. And because I was still employed, paying the bills, living in a nice (though filthy) apartment, and driving a functional automobile, I told myself I was OK.

It was all a façade, of course.

When I look back at my active addiction, the worst moment for me—the moment I least want to experience again—is a bit surprising. It doesn't involve getting arrested, or being forced into treatment, or taking a demotion at work because I'd hit a point where I was no longer able to fulfill all the duties of my job. No, my worst moment was a Christmas Eve.

As I was hitting rock bottom in pretty much every aspect of my life, my sister gave birth to her third child. To celebrate, my parents were flying to California to spend Christmas at my sister's house, and I was driving down to Orange County to join everyone. On Christmas Eve, my sister made dinner for the family and then we went to a 10 p.m. church service. After the service, rather than going back to my sister's house to sleep on the couch, I told my family I preferred to sleep in my own bed, and I'd be back in the morning for breakfast and presents. But instead of going home and getting some sleep, I got high and cruised the streets of Los Angeles looking for sex.

At 6 a.m., I finally drove home, took a shower, put on some fresh clothes, and drove back to my sister's.

There are pictures from that Christmas Eve and the following Christmas Day. My parents, my sister, her kids, and her then-husband are all there—not just physically, but emotionally. Me? Well, my body is there, but my soul is not. The photos clearly show that I am completely, totally, 100 percent disconnected from the joy of being with my family at Christmas. And in retrospect, I know it's because I did not want to be there. I wanted to be alone with my addiction. I wanted to leave.

I cheated myself that day. Worse still, I cheated the people who love and care about me. That, for me, is the nadir of my addiction. In fact, it is the nadir of my life. That is the experience that I never want to have again. That is the memory, when I need to remember why my sobriety is so important, that I turn to. Me, looking like an extra from *The Walking Dead* and wishing I was anywhere but with my own family at Christmas.

Task Two: Powerlessness Inventory

Here, addicts are generally asked to list examples, as many as possible, of their powerlessness over addictive behaviors. Basically, they list examples of their inability to stop their behavior despite obvious consequences, such as, "I was warned that if I showed up to work one more time smelling of alcohol that I would be fired, and I still stopped off at the bar for a quick drink before work."

Addicts are encouraged to be as specific as they can with this exercise, starting with early examples of powerlessness and ending with the most recent.

A few things on my powerlessness inventory are:

- Even though my car was covered in scratches and dents, I continued to drive while impaired.
- Even though my work was suffering, I continued to engage in addictive behaviors during working hours.
- Even though my friends had expressed concern about what I was doing to myself and my life, I continued my addictive behaviors.

Task Three: Unmanageability Inventory

Here, addicts are asked to list examples, as many as possible, that demonstrate how their life has become unmanageable. Basically, they list they ways in which their addiction has created chaos and destruction in their life and the lives of loved ones, such as, "I sold my car for thousands less than it was worth because I was on a meth/sex bender and needed some quick cash to pay for drugs and prostitutes."

Again, addicts are encouraged to be as specific as they can, starting with early examples of unmanageability and ending with the most recent.

A few things on my powerlessness inventory are:

- My friends and family stopped calling me because they were tired of me turning them down or canceling at the last minute so I could engage in my addiction.
- I got demoted at work because I was more focused on my addiction than my job.
- I was depressed, anxious, and had constant headaches related to addictive behaviors and the stress of living a double-life.

Task Four: Sharing Powerlessness and Unmanageability Inventories

Now comes the hardest part for most addicts: sharing their powerlessness and unmanageability inventories with their therapy group and/or their 12-Step support group. Until addicts are deeper into recovery, it is usually best that they do not share these inventories with their partner and other loved ones. In fact, this type of disclosure about the addiction should only be done in the presence of a trained addiction therapist, with significant guidance on when and how to do this disclosure (to make sure it will be helpful not only to the addict but to the loved one). For more about the process of addiction disclosure, we recommend reading *Courageous Love* by Dr. Stefanie Carnes. The book is written primarily for couples healing from sex addiction, but the principles apply to any addiction.

At this point, most addicts are overflowing with guilt, shame, remorse, and self-loathing. Plus, they've gotten very used to keeping secrets from their loved ones, their employer, and the world at large. Opening up to others about the nature and extent of their addictive behavior is anathema to their entire existence. It is completely unnatural, and they don't want to do it.

However, addicts nearly always find that sharing about their history and the consequences of their addiction helps to lift the burden of compartmentalizing their problems and lugging them around in secret. Letting go of these painful, shameful secrets frees them and allows them to move forward into a different, better life. For many addicts, the act of sharing their Step 1 inventories is the true start of recovery because it's the moment they finally decide to let others in. Many addicts say their life began to get better the moment they got honest with their recovery support network by sharing their Step 1 work.

What We Get From Step 1

At the end of the day, addicts work Step 1 to achieve *and maintain* clarity about their lives. In 12-Step meetings, addicts often talk about or hear discussion about "hitting bottom" and the resultant moment of clarity—the moment when someone finally understood and accepted that they had a major problem and needed to make significant changes. Unfortunately, these moments of clarity can be fleeting. When the crisis passes, so does the addict's desire to live differently.

This is where Step 1 comes in. Addicts work Step 1 by unearthing their complete addictive history and the problems their addiction has created. In so doing, they see, often for the first time, the totality of their addiction and its consequences. In short, they reinforce their moment of clarity and (hopefully) cement their desire for recovery and healing.

I initially shared my Step 1 work in a group therapy session, opening up to my therapist and a small group of men who had problems that were similar to my own. Becoming vulnerable in this way was not easy for me, and I did not feel the immediate sense of relief that many addicts feel when they do this. I did, however, feel that I'd at least cracked open the door to being known and finding recovery. More importantly, completing Step 1 helped to dismantle the wall of denial I'd been hiding behind for most of my adult life.

If you're a non-addict, of course, you may not identify with much that I have written about Step 1. If so, don't worry. You're not an addict, so you shouldn't, and good for you. That said, you can still benefit from Step 1 and the steps that follow. Countless non-addicts have. Kristin will explain how they've done so starting in the next section.

Step 1 for Non-Addicts

We admitted we were powerless over [some aspect of our lives]—that our lives had become unmanageable.

Although I do not identify as an addict, I've made many choices and engaged in many behaviors that have absolutely caused my life to become unmanageable. And I do not believe I'm in the minority with that. Most people have experienced powerlessness with something or someone that has led to unmanageability at some point in life. An unhealthy relationship that we didn't have the strength to end. A reaction to something that we later regretted. A compulsion to continue eating, overworking, spending, or something else, despite how much it was harming us or others. It's in these moments where we can feel powerless. That initial admission, according to Step 1, is the only requirement to begin the journey of self-exploration and growth that can be experienced through the 12-Step model.

The Obvious First Task: Determine the Problem

Step 1's process of admitting that we are powerless over some aspect (or aspects) of life is the rational first step toward change. In the most basic terms, this is saying: Just own that you have a problem, you're imperfect, and things aren't going well.

To get started, ask yourself what's not working for you anymore. If the answer comes to you quickly and easily, it's probably not the correct answer (or the complete answer), and you'll need to dig a little deeper.

This is the first of many complex and often subconscious truths that you'll need to uncover. Often, this is best accomplished with the help of a psychotherapeutic professional or a 12-Step recovery community for non-addicts, such as Al-Anon or Prodependence Anonymous.

In my own life, I only stopped and thought about what was no longer working in my world long enough to acknowledge the surface issues. For instance, I knew I felt bitter and angry about my mom's premature death, but I couldn't transcend the grief. I felt confused by my new role as a mother and a professional, but I had no idea how to reconcile my confusion. I felt hurt and betrayed by my husband's rejection, but I preferred to writhe in hatred toward him rather than working on my own shame around our marital issues. In retrospect, the pain of it all was too much to look any deeper. But there's nothing like years of hurt, pain, and suffering to trigger a deeper search for change. And that search helped me see that even my best thinking and behavior were only perpetuating further suffering and messiness—even when parts of the problem were the result of several challenging life circumstances.

During my years of struggle, I spent more energy blaming my problems on everyone and everything outside of me than in looking at my own part. After all, I could easily conjure up a long list of sob stories to explain my destructive behaviors and dysfunction: my husband's abandonment, my mom's death, feeling overwhelmed while working and raising young kids, etc. My lack of understanding of myself, what I was experiencing, and how to cope with it all created a dark storm of emotions in me. I raged and quietly considered suicide. I became possessed by my hatred toward God, cancer, my husband, and every other uncontrollable entity in my life. I questioned every relationship and everything that was formerly foundational in my life, especially love, religion, and family. I became robotic and selfish in my choices, turning my back on all of my guiding principles and values.

Ironically, if someone asked me during those years how I thought I was managing my stress and adversity I would have blindly told them I was managing it in a "normal, healthy way." However, I wasn't, and the abrupt dismantling of my marriage triggered the final blow that launched me into full self-destruction mode.

As I began to study the 12 Steps as part of my training as an addiction therapist, I saw that Step 1 was extremely applicable to me because I'd lost control over my life—my faculties, my values, my goals, my entire life's path after a string of difficult events, and, as a result of that, my life had become unmanageable. In short, I was *powerless over my poor coping skills* and entirely *unable to manage the vulnerabilities of my life.*

How to Determine What's Not Working for You

Below are a few indicators that you may be powerless to start a healthy behavior or stop an unhealthy behavior, and you can't make the desired change without help.

- Do you talk to yourself, making promises to yourself or others that today you're going to (fill in the blank), but then end up behaving the same as you always do?
- Do you talk to yourself, making promises to yourself or others that today you're *not* going to (fill in the blank), but then end up behaving the same as you always do?

Probing the Pain to Find the Problem

One of the most mind-blowing (and frustrating) truths I've uncovered during my years in the helping profession is that humans—all the way down to a cellular level—only tend to change and grow when faced with intense discomfort, pain, or adversity. If I ever get a chance to talk to my Higher Power, I want to ask why we were created with this deeply confusing, counterintuitive design. Why do we only seem to really learn and grow when we are struggling and challenged?

About this conundrum, Richard Rohr writes in *Breathing Under Water*:

> Until you bottom out and come to the limits of your own fuel supply, there is no reason for you to switch to a higher octane of fuel. ... You will not learn to actively draw upon a Larger Source until your usual resources are depleted. ... In fact, you will not even know there is a Larger Source until your own sources and resources fail you.

Our psyches have amazing coping skills and defense mechanisms that distract us from our daily discomfort. We can easily drink the pain away, blame it on others, or seek temporary relief and escape with sex, relationships, spending, eating, or performing/achieving. This is exactly why Step 1 is paramount to growth and change. Can we sit with the pain long enough to identify what is no longer working so we can then take purposeful steps to try to change it? If we can, we have a chance to eliminate our pain instead of temporarily escaping it.

Can we sit with the pain long enough to identify what is no longer working so we can then take purposeful steps to try to change it? If we can, we have a chance to eliminate our pain instead of temporarily escaping it.

Owning Our Powerlessness Creates Strength

It is important to realize that owning that we are powerless does not mean that we are helpless. Nevertheless, our ego and pride often get in the way of Step 1 because our instinct is to avoid change, even if the current situation isn't working. Instead of changing, we continue to do what doesn't work, thinking that the next time will be different.

It's in these moments of unmanageability that we need to find a new manager. In *Breathing Under Water* Rohr asserts:

> Addicts develop a love and trust relationship with a substance or compulsion of some kind, [and this] becomes their primary emotional relationship with life itself. This is a god who cannot save. It is momentary intensity passing for the intimacy they really want, and it is always quickly over.

Addicts or not, we all behave in this way. We seek out external sources to validate us, to help us escape from pain or discomfort, and to help us feel like we're "good enough." The temporary relief mechanisms we use inevitably lead us to the addict's definition of insanity: doing the same thing over and over but expecting different results. The obvious (but scary) path to freedom from this insanity cycle is to admit that what you're doing is no longer working, that your best thinking got you here, and that you need to make some significant life changes. For me, I needed to stop expending all of my energy and focus on hating others, and I needed to stop using unfortunate circumstances in my life as entitlement to be selfish, vengeful, and to engage in unhealthy, escapist behaviors. I had to own that I was floundering desperately and needed help to stop my toxic cycle.

It is perfectly natural to fight this, however. As human beings, we do not want to admit that we are powerless. We do not want to admit that our lives are unmanageable. We do not want to surrender to anything, because the mere idea of surrender causes us to feel even more powerless and less able to manage our lives. But surrender we must.

When told about the need to surrender, both addicts and non-addicts immediately think that surrendering means their problem (whatever that problem might be) has beaten them and they cannot overcome it no matter how hard they try, so they might as well give up. But that is not what is meant by surrender in this context. The surrender that is asked for in Step 1 is not in any way an admission of permanent defeat at the hands of the problem. In fact, we do not need to surrender to the problem at all. Instead, we surrender to *reality*—most notably, *the reality of having a problem* that we need to deal with. When we surrender to the reality of having a problem, we can then take steps to address that problem.

Interestingly, as 12-Step healing progresses, most of us find that the concept of surrender extends well beyond the initially identified problem. This is best described in the book *Alcoholics Anonymous*, which states:

> When I am disturbed, it is because I find some person, place, or situation—some fact of my life—unacceptable to me, and I can find no serenity until I accept that person, place, thing, or situation as being exactly the way it is supposed to be at this moment. ... Unless I accept life completely on life's terms, I cannot be happy. I need to concentrate not so much on what needs to be changed in the world as on what needs to be changed in me and in my attitudes.

This passage was initially written to help alcoholics learn to accept life on life's terms as part of staying sober, but it applies to every recovering addict, regardless of the nature of the addiction, and every non-addict, too.

We need to accept that we cannot control the thinking and

behavior of any person other than ourselves. Sure, we can set healthy boundaries around the behavior of others to protect ourselves, but we cannot control their choices. They will think what they think and do what they do, and there is nothing we can do about it.

In this life, all that we really have control over is ourselves. The only thing we can change is ourselves. And much of the time, the easiest thing to change about ourselves is our attitude toward the choices that other people make. To do this, we need to surrender to our lack of control over people, places, things, and situations that upset us. We must learn to place more value on peace and serenity than on being right—even when we're 100 percent certain we're right.

Before my experience with 12 Steps, I felt completely incapable of accepting life on life's terms. I drove myself insane worrying about things over which I had no control. Instead of coming to terms with my powerlessness, I would numb, blame, distract from, and rage, hoping those behaviors would magically change my reality. Once I was able to acknowledge that my semi-intelligent, determined, controlling, and prideful self still ended up sad, angry, scared, and struggling, I was able to surrender and accept a new system for change—a new manager. And with that help, I began to find answers that I, alone, could not find.

Step 1, Exercise 1: Identifying Problems

For non-addicts, specifically and accurately identifying what needs to change can be difficult. This is especially true for non-addicts who are in relationship with an addict. In such cases (and a lot of other cases), it is very easy (and natural) for the non-addict to shift the onus for all problems onto the addict. And why not, when the addict has a clear and obvious problem that's accompanied by *lots* of bad behavior.

Under no circumstances should non-addicts take blame for choices other people have made—especially not the choices made by addicted loved ones. Each person makes his or her own choices. Period. So, rather than focusing on what the people around you have done and how their behavior has impacted you, focus on what you have done and continue to do and how your choices and behaviors have impacted your life.

Without thinking too much, list ten things that bother you or upset you. Example: I spend too much money on things I don't really need.

1. ______________________________
2. ______________________________
3. ______________________________
4. ______________________________
5. ______________________________
6. ______________________________
7. ______________________________
8. ______________________________
9. ______________________________
10. ______________________________

Now examine each item on the list of things that bother or upset you and look for your part in it—how your choices and behavior have perpetuated, facilitated, or even caused the problem. Do not take blame for the behavior of others. Simply look for choices you've made and behaviors you've engaged in that, in some way, play into you feeling bothered or upset. In the space below, for each item listed above, list your part.

1. ____
2. ____
3. ____
4. ____
5. ____
6. ____
7. ____
8. ____
9. ____
10. ____

Does anything about your own choices and behavior pop out as particularly troublesome? Do you people please? Try to control and manipulate? Live in fear? Avoid difficult conversations and decisions? If so, write a paragraph about this, and how you feel about it.

____

____

____

____

____

Step 1, Exercise 2: Powerlessness and Unmanageability

The initial work in all 12-step recovery programs involves an admission that you are powerless over some problem in your life, and that problem has caused your life to become unmanageable.

- **Powerless** means you have lost control over the problem (whatever it happens to be). You engage in behaviors even when you say you don't want to. You show minimal ability to stop these behaviors once you've started. Powerlessness means that despite the promises you've made to yourself and/or others that you are going to stop a certain behavior, you find yourself right back at it.
- **Unmanageable** speaks primarily to the consequences of the behavior over which you are powerless. These consequences can be both direct (obviously connected) and indirect (less obviously connected).

List ten examples of your powerlessness. Use the following format: Even though I (list a particular consequence), I continued to (list a particular behavior). Example: Even though I continue to feel bad for screaming at my kids and make promises to do better, I continue to lose my temper and scream at them.

1. ____

____

2. ____

____

3. ____

____

4. ____

____

5. ____

____

6. __________

____

7. __________

____

8. __________

____

9. __________

____

10. __________

____

List ten examples of unmanageability (problems and consequences) related to your problem behavior. Example: I continually escalate disagreements with my children by yelling and losing my temper, saying things I don't mean to say, and failing to take breaks to calm down.

1. __________

____

2. __________

____

3. __________

____

4. __________

____

5. __________

____

6. __________

7.

8.

9.

10.

Do you feel that you are powerless over some of your behaviors and, as a result, that parts of your life have become unmanageable? If so, how do you feel about that?

Step 1, Exercise 3: Identifying and Establishing Values and Goals

Identifying your values and goals is an essential first step on your journey to change. Values and goals can act as your roadmap through life, helping you decide the healthiest steps forward. It's easier to make decisions and navigate through relationships and difficult situations when you are clear on your values and goals. It is not a therapist's or a sponsor's job to tell you what you should or shouldn't do with your life. However, a therapist or sponsor can help you remain accountable once you convey your values and goals to them.

Values:	Goals:	Aspirational Goals:
Moral principles or desired qualities. Flexible guidelines that we choose freely. They are not something to achieve but may influence the path you take. Dr. Brené Brown, defines values as "a way of being or belief that you hold most important."	The object of your ambition or effort; an aim or desired result. Goals are formed by values and are aligned with your values, though sometimes values and goals can conflict (cognitive dissonance). Goals are things you pursue with the future in mind.	These are externally driven. These are a hope or ambition of achieving something.

Please answer the following questions.

What do you choose to do to fill your free time and why? What are your hobbies or creative outlets? How do these behaviors serve you?

What kind of things do you try to do daily or on a regular basis? Why?

What do you love doing?

What do you dream of doing? How do you wish you could spend your days and free time?

How do you define yourself or how would you like to be described by others?

What qualities in others do you most appreciate and admire?

___

___

___

List ten personal *values, beliefs, or qualities* (about yourself) that are important to you. These can be things you aspire to be or things you already feel you are. Examples: I am athletic; I am smart; I want to be financially successful.

1. ___
2. ___
3. ___
4. ___
5. ___
6. ___
7. ___
8. ___
9. ___
10. ___

List five things you want to change about yourself. Example: I can be selfish sometimes.

1. ___
2. ___
3. ___
4. ___
5. ___

What are your three biggest goals that you want to complete this year? These can be personal, familial, professional, physical, mental, emotional, spiritual, etc.

1. ______________________________
2. ______________________________
3. ______________________________

What are three goals you'd like to complete in the next five years? These can be personal, familial, professional, physical, mental, emotional, spiritual, etc.

1. ______________________________
2. ______________________________
3. ______________________________

List up to three life dreams that you want to fulfill before you die?

1. ______________________________
2. ______________________________
3. ______________________________

What role, if any, does religion/spirituality play in your life?

1. ______________________________
2. ______________________________
3. ______________________________

What behaviors do you engage in to practice your values? How are you moving toward your goals?

1. ______________________________

2. ______________________________
3. ______________________________

What things are getting in the way of your values and goals? These can be cultural, familial, social, logistical, etc.

1. ______________________________
2. ______________________________
3. ______________________________

Tim vs. Will

Two clients, Tim and Will, entered therapy at the same time with similar stories. Both were in their mid-40s, good-looking, successful business owners, and expressing depression along with some substance use issues. Both were sent to therapy after their wives uncovered extramarital affairs.

While in therapy, Will came clean to his wife about all of his transgressions, was willing to engage in months of uncomfortable work, sharing shameful stories and owning the harm that he caused his loved ones due to his affairs and substance use. Will was willing to humble himself to the uncomfortable process of coming clean about all the things he'd done while developing and implementing an accountability structure to help him stay on a healthy path of healing and honesty.

The other client, Tim, was the opposite of Will. Tim resisted engaging in therapy. In lieu of owning his mistakes and shortcomings, he had a lot of justifications and rationalizations for his cheating and substance use. He rarely owned his part in the toxic cycle with his estranged wife, often saying things like "She never loved me anyway" or "We just aren't meant to be together." He continued to lie and engage in substance abuse and inappropriate relationships with other women.

A full year later, Will and Tim were in very different places mentally, emotionally, professionally, and in their relationships. Will, who humbled himself, reported his marriage was stronger and better than he could have imagined. He felt grateful to keep his family intact while also experiencing love for the first time because his wife finally knew everything he'd done and still forgave him and continued to work on healing with him.

Tim, on the other hand, returned to treatment worse than before. His wife had left him and his kids were mad at him. He reported that his depression and suicidal thoughts had worsened and his business was failing. He continued to abuse substances and engage in casual sex with many women, including some who were married. In therapy, it was obvious that he continued to drown in shame and wouldn't find relief until he began owning what wasn't working for him.

Getting honest. Asking for help. Accepting influence. Similar stories, two very different outcomes. The biggest difference being Will's willingness to own that life wasn't working for him, that his life had become unmanageable, while Tim continued to minimize his behaviors, blame others, and pretend that things would just get better on their own. Will did the work of Step 1. Tim did not. Will got better. Tim did not.

Step 2 for Addicts

Came to believe that a power greater than ourselves could restore us to sanity.

For addicts, thoroughly working Step 2—coming to believe that a power greater than themselves will restore them to sanity—is vital to recovery because it prepares them for the longer-term solution to come. It introduces them to the idea that they must accept outside assistance and guidance if they want to establish and maintain sobriety. They've tried it on their own and they couldn't stay sober, so now they're going to have to rely on something greater than themselves (a process that takes place in Steps 3 through 12).

Step 2 asks:

- Did you continue with addictive behavior even though it was creating problems?
- Did you try and repeatedly fail to cut back or quit your addictive behavior?
- Did these attempts and failures to cut back or quit happen more than once?

For addicts, if they're able to be honest, the answer to all three of these questions will be yes. That was certainly the case for me. Typically, addicts have tried to quit on their own—multiple times—but they can't seem to stay sober for more than a few days, despite the (usually escalating) series of problems their addiction creates. Their best thinking and best efforts were not enough to change their behavior. As such, any lasting solution to their problem must involve something beyond themselves. Helping addicts understand and accept the need for outside assistance is the purpose of Step 2.

Of course, most addicts would rather eat a plate of worms than ask for help. This resistance is partly the human condition, partly the disease. Overcoming it is vital to healing. Often, when addicts new to 12-Step recovery struggle with this, they are asked to simply sit back and watch others in the program. In so doing, they can't help but see at least a few people who are no longer active in their addiction, no longer behaving in problematic ways, and no longer experiencing serious life consequences as a result. And almost all of those recovering individuals, if asked, will say that they did not establish or maintain their sobriety on their own. Instead, they reached out for and accepted the help of others. In other words, they worked Step 2.

A desire to recover on their own, without help, is not the only issue that addicts have with Step 2. Addicts also struggle with the closing words of this step, "restore us to sanity," as this phrase suggests they are insane, and they rarely think that's the case. If someone else was engaging in the same behaviors as them, sure, that person would be totally nuts, but somehow, addicts nearly always feel that their own behavior is reasonable and normal. And they have a hundred different justifications, rationalizations, and explanations for that misguided belief.

Typically, when addicts struggle with the being crazy concept, their therapist, their 12-Step sponsor, or friends in recovery will explain to them the addict's definition of insanity, which is doing the same things over and over but expecting different results. These individuals will say something like, "The last hundred times you went out for a drink, you couldn't stop. Every time, you kept drinking until something bad happened (hangover, wreck, argument, fight, arrest, etc.). But this time you think you'll have just one cocktail and toddle home unscathed? Yes, good luck with that. And good luck convincing yourself that continuing to drink the way you always drink is not insanity."

Other addicts struggle with the words "power greater than ourselves," interpreting that language to mean "God" or "organized religion." But this is not what it means. Instead, these words typically refer to a mix of things like 12-Step recovery groups, supportive friends and family, therapists and therapy groups, and the like. For some people, traditional concepts of God and religion also enter the mix; for plenty of others, not so much. At the end of the day, a recovering addict's definition of "power greater than ourselves" depends as much on the individual's personal belief system as anything else. For addicts, Step 2 is less about God/religion/spirituality and more about admitting that help is needed.

All that is needed for addicts to work Step 2 is to recognize and accept they need help from a power greater than themselves. The good news is that there is no right or wrong way to define that power. If addicts choose to include a formalized version of God and religion in their definition of "power greater than ourselves," that's great. If not, they can think about 12-Step fellowships, therapists, loved ones, and others who support their recovery as that power. When Step 2 is worked, addicts recognize that they need to start trusting others and becoming accountable because, as they have repeatedly proven through failed efforts to change on their own, accepting outside help is essential to long-term recovery.

Step 2 for Non-Addicts

Came to believe that a power greater than ourselves could restore us to sanity.

As non-addicts, with Step 1 we determine we are struggling and things are no longer working in our life. Once the problem or problems have been defined and laid out, we can move on to Step 2, coming *to believe that a power greater than ourselves can restore us to sanity.*

This seems relatively logical. After all, owning the fact that our life has become unmanageable will hopefully lead us to *seek help from a source outside of our own best thinking.* Our best efforts and attempts to limit our exposure to harm have led us to our current state of struggle, and it no longer makes sense to go it alone.

Unfortunately, we humans don't always do what makes sense, especially when we're faced with crisis and suffering.

Step 2 sounds basic, but allowing it to seep deep into our soul is a complicated process. Our default state is to control, predict, and protect ourselves (and our loved ones) from the uncertainty and chaos of the world. The idea of trusting another source for help in a time of crisis is counterintuitive. After all, we're highly adaptive creatures. We spend most of our lives using our traits and talents to survive and thrive in a vulnerable world. These traits and talents allow us to gain attention, connection, success, and more.

Our default state is to control, predict, and protect ourselves (and our loved ones) from the uncertainty and chaos of the world. The idea of trusting another source for help in a time of crisis is counterintuitive.

Something to Ponder: What are Your Traits and Talents?

Look back on your childhood and early adulthood. When did you receive attention, both negative and positive? Was it for being the responsible one, for being stable and not having many needs? Was it for being athletic? For academic performance? For being a rebel or class clown?

As long as things *appear* to be working for us, we'll continue to use our traits and talents to create a false sense of control in an uncontrollable world. It is only when we realize that our life (or some important aspect of our life) has reached a level of powerlessness and unmanageability—despite the use of our best traits and talents—that we are compelled to seek another source to restore sanity: a power greater than ourselves.

At this point, you may ask: Does a "power greater than myself" have to be a spiritual Higher Power (i.e., a divine source or deity)? My answer is that it must be something more than another flawed human being or an external, inanimate source like drugs, alcohol, food, money, success, looks, etc. The Higher Power we turn to for help must be higher than our own power and our own will to control and manipulate our lives (and the lives of others). But as Scott states in his explanation of Step 2 for addicts, we needn't define that Higher Power at this early stage. The goal of Step 2 is simply that we find the willingness to accept help from a power outside ourselves.

That said, worldly power and willpower are fleeting and broken. A Higher Power is consistent and whole. Finding grounding in a Higher Power brings us a sense of security that helps us navigate the insecurities of life. Thus, a foundational spiritual practice (whatever that looks like for each of us) provides us with the stability needed to weather the storm of uncertainty, shame, and suffering.

Inviting a Higher Power into our healing process can prove difficult, depending on our level of spiritual exposure throughout our life. It can take many years and great difficulty to overcome our defenses, get in touch with our "shame voices," and give up attempts to control, manage, and perpetuate the cycle of our insanity (our tendency to do the same thing over and over while expecting different results). But we must do this work if we hope to reach a deeper, soul-level change.

I can appreciate the complexity of Step 2 as much as anyone because I was very anti-Higher Power when I was in my personal crisis. I was angry and felt let down by my version of God, and I didn't want to "need" a Higher Power. However, my pain and discomfort were extreme enough for me to acknowledge my powerlessness and unmanageability. With that realization, it became abundantly clear that everything I had done to that point was not working. I was making surface-level behavioral changes, but nothing was penetrating deeply enough to change the way I viewed the world and my problems. Thus, I was unable to find relief from my misery.

As non-addicts explore Step 2, it's important to identify the great disparity between behavioral changes (I call this "The Grocery

List of Things I Should be Doing") and deeper, more meaningful, soul-level changes. Behavioral changes are like band-aids on a wound. Yes, band-aids serve a necessary function, but they are not the most important part of the healing process. Band-aids are a surface fix that can assist in the healing process, but the bulk of the work occurs from within, over time.

Richard Rohr beautifully explains that behavioral changes are for those *avoiding hell*, while deeper soul-level changes are experienced by those who have *been through hell*. Step 2 is for people who've been through hell.

Two Types of Change

We have different meanings and approaches to change. Some religions call it salvation. Addicts call it recovery. Either way, the individuals involved feel a deep need to explore their past to change their future.

I've had a lot of clients recently and in the past who've had years of abstaining from drugs or alcohol coupled with years of attending AA or some other recovery community, but they're still "acting out" in other ways. They're still using others; they're still raging at their spouse; they're still passive-aggressive and resentful or just plain old miserable in or out of their relationships. Have these individuals changed in meaningful ways? Yes, probably. But one could argue that they're still not living a life in recovery. In other words, not enough has changed.

Working with addicts trying to recover, I've seen that there are two different levels of change.

1. Behavioral Change
2. Spiritual/Emotional/Soulful Change

The first level of change, behavioral change, alters the way we act, the choices we make, the things we "do." If I'm an alcoholic, the most obvious behavioral change I need to make is to stop drinking.

That's the first layer of change that must happen. However, while behavioral changes are a necessary function, they are not the most important part of the healing process. The most important part is the change that occurs internally. The good news is that surface changes can contribute to the deeper, soulful change, as long as one continues to explore the problems and issues beneath the surface behaviors.

Addicts in recovery call surface changes "white-knuckling," meaning they're using willpower and little else to stay sober. In AA, individuals who white-knuckle their way to sobriety are considered "dry drunks." Dry drunks may stop drinking, but they resist the deeper, more complicated work of figuring out what led them to chronically drink in the first place. Their deeper issues remain unacknowledged and unprocessed. As a consequence, they continue to behave like addicts, but without the alcohol. They're still controlling and highly defensive. They continue to lie, manipulate, and avoid conflict. Often, their sobriety is short-lived.

I have watched countless addicts go to treatment, attend therapy groups, go to 12-Step meetings, stop drinking, and understandably claim to be sober. However, it doesn't take long to know whether they've only made behavioral (surface) changes or if the process of healing has sunk deeper, changing the way they think, feel, connect, and experience life. That second layer of change is the emotional/spiritual/soulful change that both addicts and non-addicts seek. And that second layer of change only begins when we fully explore Step 2.

Step 2, Exercise 1: Identifying Our Superpowers and Curses

We are controlling, adaptive beings by nature. Our long list of traits and talents are proof that we can learn special skills to gain the attention (good or bad) that we require. However, as we begin to work Step 2 and realize that we need to surrender to a new manager, it's important to reflect on the behaviors and tactics we've used to navigate our lives up until this point.

This exercise helps you identify and explore the traits and behaviors you adopted as a consequence of your environment and reinforcement from others. It is interesting to realize that many of the traits and talents that we have today were things we got a lot of attention for as we were growing up (positive or negative).

Our traits and talents serve a purpose, but we may have been limiting ourselves by not allowing ourselves to also engage in the "opposite" behaviors. For instance, if I was valued in my family system and at school for being a rule-follower or hyper-organized, I might struggle with any form of rule-breaking, non-conformity, or messiness. If I got a lot of attention for being the class clown, I might struggle with allowing myself to be sad or serious.

The following exercise helps us to identify traits and talents that we value about ourselves in addition to "lost" parts of ourselves that we'd like to adopt and bring into our current relationships. This exercise may also be a helpful tool in working Steps 6 and 7. Please take a few moments to fill in the following chart. Your responses will help you to better understand and take in the remainder of this book.

Exploring Our Childhood, Our "Lost Self", and Shame

Ways you received validation & attention from friends, family, authority figures growing up	The opposite of that behavior or characteristic (What you couldn't be):	Parts of your "Lost Self" you'd like to reclaim:

Step 2, Exercise 2: Band-Aids vs. Deeper Healing

As you examine your life, you'll see many obvious things you'd like to fix. These are surface level behavioral changes. But are you willing to look underneath the surface manifestations to see what drives your problem thinking and behaviors? Are you willing to make the second level spiritual/emotional/soulful changes?

We certainly hope you are willing to make the deeper changes. If you're not, you will not improve your life in the ways you might hope. This exercise is designed to help you identify, first, the obvious surface level changes you'd like to make, and then to look beneath the surface in ways that might uncover some (though by no means all) of the deeper changes you would like to make.

In the space below, list five surface level behavioral changes you would like to make. Example: I would like to stop screaming at my children when I get frustrated or overwhelmed.

1. ______________________________
2. ______________________________
3. ______________________________
4. ______________________________
5. ______________________________

Now, for each behavior you'd like to change, list a feeling, a belief that you hold about yourself, and a thought that supports that behavior. Example: When I scream at my children, it's because I'm feeling overwhelmed.

1. ______________________________
2. ______________________________
3. ______________________________
4. ______________________________

5. ____

Are you willing to change not only the surface level behaviors but the corresponding feelings, beliefs, and thoughts? Please write about this in the space below. Example: When I feel myself losing my temper, I need to slow down, better understand what I'm really upset about, and find more productive ways of expressing my feelings.

____

____

____

____

____

Josie vs. the Old Man with a Long White Beard

Josie was a single, straight, 30-something producer in the entertainment industry. She worked long hours and spent a lot of time on the road. Despite a desire to get married and have a family, her behaviors and choices looked like a regular pattern of "sexting" random men while traveling for business, meeting up with men for casual sex, and viewing porn. She expressed values of wanting to engage men in a more intimate, vulnerable way, and to not use sexual encounters as a way to stave off boredom and loneliness. She would go through seasons of swearing off sexting, hooking up, or using porn in an effort to "be better." Then, the nights in the hotels would get lonely or the "still moments" back at home would become untenable and the cycle would begin again.

Josie was raised in a family with a strict Catholic upbringing. "I believed there was an old guy with a white beard who gets really mad when I do something wrong but is happy when I do something right," she said. "I feel like I'm always being watched and judged. And that I'm always failing."

Josie's exploration of how much her religious upbringing and the values (and fears) instilled in her contributed to her unhealthy patterns around sex, fears of intimacy, and chronic shame. The Higher Power Josie was raised with made her feel wrong, bad, and like no one could accept her if they really knew her, especially when it came to her sexual history.

Josie's view of a Higher Power was damaging, so she had to find a Higher Power that would help her heal and work toward healthier, intimate relationships with herself and others. When asked to write out what she would really want her Higher Power to be, she found that the traits were someone she would want as a close friend. Someone who doesn't judge but loves her and wants the best for her. Someone who doesn't care how much money she makes or what she does sexually. Someone who wants to spend time with her and talk with her.

Josie's Step 2 work triggered change in all areas of her life: her relationships, health, finances, sexuality, emotions, and spirituality. "It's a simple program," Josie concludes, "but nothing about it is easy."

Step Three for Addicts

Made a decision to turn our will and our lives over to the care of God as we understood God.

Step 1 helps addicts understand the depth and consequences of their addiction. Step 2 helps them see that if they hope to make changes for the better, outside help is needed. Step 3 starts the process of actually accepting that help. In this way, Step 3 is the first "action step" of recovery, as it is the first time that addicts are asked to actually do something: They are asked to *make a decision* that outside guidance will be accepted and followed.

For many addicts, in particular those who have a good working relationship with the religion or spiritual practices of their childhood, or who've developed a religious or spiritual practice as adults with which they are comfortable and confident, Step 3 is relatively easy. They simply turn to what they already know and believe in. For others, however, Step 3 is not so simple. It is not unusual for the word "God" to bungle the works a bit, as many addicts have bad memories of the punishing deity with which they were raised. You know: tall guy, white beard, flowing robes, gets really, really angry when we don't do exactly what he wants, when he wants, and then he drops a plague of locusts or floods the planet or does something else that sort of seems like overkill. Plenty of addicts, even those who are eager for recovery, have no intention whatsoever of ever re-engaging with that guy.

Well, good news: That's not what Step 3 is about. For addicts who struggle with "the God thing," it is perfectly acceptable to substitute the words used in Step 2, "power greater than ourselves." Believing in a traditional version of God and understanding a traditional version of God are not necessary for recovery. Addicts only need to decide that they need and will accept outside help, which usually arrives in the form of supportive real-world people who can aid in their ongoing sobriety—therapists, 12-Step fellowships, 12-Step sponsors, friends in recovery, etc. For many recovering addicts the word God becomes an acronym for the "Good Orderly Direction" given by their advisors and support network.

Nevertheless, some addicts still struggle mightily with the God thing. The religion of their early life is simply too ingrained and the resentments run too deep. In such cases, a simple exercise often helps. First, addicts get a large sheet of paper. On it, they draw a giant circle. Inside the circle they write attributes that they think their ideal Higher Power would possess—loving, caring, honest, funny, protective, nurturing, etc. Outside the circle, they write attributes that their Higher Power should not possess—angry, judgmental, punishing, dictatorial, and the like. Then they use a pair of scissors to cut away whatever is outside the circle. These undesirable attributes are then ripped up and thrown away, ceremonially burned, or whatever. Addicts then agree to *act as if* what remains, the desirable Higher Power attributes, are the reality of God *for them*.

Another option is to write a job description. To do this, addicts should ask:

- What do I want from a Higher Power?
- How can I learn to trust this Higher Power?
- What sort of interactive give and take between me and my Higher Power should occur?

Sometimes it helps to write a want-ad.

> *Sought: A power greater than myself to help me stay sober. Must be readily available and care about my health and well-being. Must understand the nature of my addiction. Must be nonjudgmental about my past. Sense of humor helpful.*

Once a Higher Power has been hired, addicts can begin the process of accepting help from that power—help that is typically delivered via a 12-Step fellowship, a sponsor, a therapist, friends in recovery, and the like. Very often this starts with simple accountability. For instance, an addict might agree to attend a 12-Step meeting five times per week, to check in with his or her sponsor on a daily basis, and to immediately call a supportive person in recovery anytime he or she has thoughts of relapse. Usually, it takes addicts very little time to realize that accepting help from a power greater than themselves, whatever that power looks like, is a good idea because doing so makes staying sober much, much easier.

When addicts think these Higher Power exercises sound silly, they are typically asked to re-read the final five words of Step 3, "God as we understood God." In other words, it is up to the addict to understand (or not understand) his or her Higher Power, and nobody in 12-Step recovery should ever judge the addict's or anyone else's concept thereof. Addicts are free to find and include in their lives any Higher Power that works *for them*, and that Higher Power need not match anyone else's in their program of recovery (or anywhere else, for that matter).

For addicts who are unwilling to consider any sort of spiritual entity, 12-Step recovery still works. In such cases, an easy way to work Step 3 is to identify three or more people that the addict is willing to trust and to ask for help with absolutely anything. Those people can form the addict's Higher Power—the collective entity to whom the addict will (at least for now) turn over willful behavior and control. Essentially, these individuals serve as sounding boards, advisors, and accountability partners.

In the end, addicts are well served to understand that a Higher Power (whether they choose to call it God or something else) can be anything outside of themselves that helps them stay sober. As such, they are not tied to any particular definitions or beliefs; instead, they are free to choose any version of a Higher Power that works *for them*, regardless of how others may feel about it.

Addicts are well served to understand that a Higher Power (whether they choose to call it God or something else) can be anything outside of themselves that helps them stay sober.

Step 3 is incredibly important in the process of recovery, because when addicts finally start to accept outside help, they are ready to move forward with the "change steps" of 12-Step recovery—Steps 4 through 9. Those are the steps where addicts actively examine their lives, see themselves as they really are, make amends, and begin the process of living differently. And those steps cannot be effectively worked without guidance, support, and faith in some type of Higher Power.

Step 3 for Non-Addicts

Made a decision to turn our will and our lives over to the care of God as we understood God.

Recovering addicts are almost universally familiar with the Serenity Prayer, as it is widely used to both open and close 12-Step meetings. But this incredibly useful prayer is hardly the sole province of recovering addicts. Countless non-addicts also know and use this prayer.

> *God, grant me serenity to accept the things I cannot change,*
> *Courage to change the things I can,*
> *And wisdom to know the difference.*

I actually had the Serenity Prayer posted up on my corkboard growing up. I didn't realize it was widely used by the 12-Step community until decades later. I just thought it sounded nice and made sense as a guide to living.

As a lifelong (and exhausted) control freak, I remember being drawn to the allure of what the Serenity Prayer suggested. I remember thinking how lovely it would be to allow myself, for once, to relinquish control to a Higher Power, to let go of the steering wheel and move over to the passenger seat for a while. I remember also thinking that relinquishing control sounded like both paradise and a nightmare. Sure, letting my Higher Power take the wheel might provide some form of relief, but it would also expose me to the chaos and uncertainty of a crazy world—chaos and uncertainty that I wanted to believe were somehow preventable or manipulatable by my own will and behavior.

So, I happily welcomed the Serenity Prayer when I found myself feeling hurt, rejected, or like a failure, but I quickly forgot about it when I was feeling on top of things (when I was feeling in control of my life and the world around me). At those times, I was determined to remain in the driver's seat, believing that as long as I had my hand on the steering wheel and I was driving down some known path, I was protecting myself from the uncertainties of life.

Unfortunately, the harder I held on to that wheel and the faster I charged down my chosen freeway, the more exhausted, fearful, ashamed, and resentful I became. My attempts at controlling and mitigating my risk got me nowhere. Well, nowhere that provided authentic peace, joy, and contentment.

That is why (only in retrospect and after years of personal work) I have been able to find gratitude for my countless trials and tribulations. Faced with a string of personal crises that brought me to my knees, I was finally able to hear the true context of Step 3 and the Serenity Prayer. I was finally able to understand that turning my will and my life over to the care of my Higher Power meant turning over *all* of my life and will, not just the parts I didn't want to control on my own. So simple, so liberating, yet completely lost on me for a very long time.

Humans love the illusion of control. Yet there's one truth I've had verified time and time again in both my personal and professional life: The most controlling people are the most miserable people. On the outside, they often look like they're winning the game of life. They are commonly the ones with financial and professional success. They look like they've got it together. Their relationships seem ideal. But this is only because they are controlling the optics of it all. They expend so much time and energy on controlling what others see and think about them that they forget to enjoy themselves.

In *Breathing Under Water*, Richard Rohr writes:

> We each have our inner program for happiness, our plans by which we can be secure, esteemed, and in control, and [we] are blissfully unaware that these cannot work for us for the long haul without our becoming more and more control freaks ourselves. ... [This] does not create happy people, nor happy people around us.

Yes, we can do our best to monitor our emotions, to vet our reactions to life's ups and downs, and to choose healthy coping skills, but we will never be able to control any other person or any event that happens beyond our personal being. Every moment we try to predict and control life by manipulating our circumstances or denying our truth, we are exhausting ourselves, continuing our suffering, and avoiding the true work of life: surrendering that which we cannot control and choosing to show up and be seen by others as our true selves (owning our good and bad, our light and dark).

Examining Control

As we explore Step 3, it's important to explore how control manifests. The first thing to know is that control can be subconscious and insidious. For example, addiction and other maladaptive coping skills are forms of controlling behaviors.

Let me explain: We are neurobiologically wired to want to connect with other humans. We aren't built to go it alone. However, we also have to face a scary world where people hurt us and bad stuff happens. Experiencing early-life trauma magnifies this subconscious fear. As a consequence, we develop traits, talents, and skills to manage our fear and discomfort related to our need to connect with others. We create a protective façade to mitigate our exposure to uncertainty.

These go-to traits, talents, and skills are our drugs of choice. They may be shots of vodka, hits from a vape, casual/anonymous sex, masturbating to porn, eating too much chocolate cake, over-working, compulsive spending, or some other form of emotional and psychological escape. They might also manifest as some form of control, such as isolation, manipulation, people-pleasing, etc. The list goes on and on.

Either way, these are superficial ways we seek control in a world that is uncertain and filled with flawed people. We try to control our emotions or we try to control others and the world at large. And we do this to manage our vulnerability instead of facing it so we can get the support we really need. We become control freaks because we are afraid of being hurt.

These go-to coping skills (ways of controlling or at least managing our inner and outer worlds), no matter how destructive they become, are sought out and used by us all, desperately and sometimes compulsively. And each of these traits, talents, and coping mechanisms works until it doesn't.

Surrender Remains Elusive Until We're in Crisis

Before my own personal crises shook me awake, I would have asserted to all that I was entirely "enough" and that I wasn't a control freak. I would have told you I had zero issues in the confidence department, and shame had no presence in my daily thought process. I would have said that I did not need any help from a Higher Power. I would have said, "I'm intelligent and resourceful. I have a loving family. I'm attractive. I'm religious-ish. I'm good."

But when push came to shove and those areas of my life became shaky, I realized my confidence and grounded-ness were an illusion. I realized I only felt smart and accomplished when bosses or friends validated me, so I would bust my ass to the point of exhaustion with hopes of getting that recognition. I felt attractive only when the scale told me I weighed a certain number of pounds, so I would restrict what I ate and relentlessly work out so I could look (and therefore feel) a certain way. And I definitely only felt like a good parent when I gave the impression that I was a calm, cool, collected mom who tirelessly and selflessly put her kids' needs first (which was not the reality).

My ego was so fragile that I couldn't hear "opportunity for growth" from anyone without getting highly defensive. I gave the outward perception that I was confident and stable, but all of my confidence and stability was built on fleeting and flawed worldly measurements that ebbed and flowed in life. Without a Higher Power, I had nothing to ground me, and that lack of self-worth manifested in my struggling mental health and relationships.

I gave the outward perception that I was confident and stable, but all of my confidence and stability was built on fleeting and flawed worldly measurements that ebbed and flowed in life.

For better or worse, we often realize how stable or unstable our identities, value, and worth are only when they're taken from us or placed in a questionable light. We can use all the controlling, helpful, evidence-based formulas and tools at our disposal to structure our lives to withstand day-to-day challenges. But when major life-altering crises hit, the reliability and fortitude of our beings will be fully tested and likely found inadequate—often because they're built on an insecure foundation.

We try to control, manipulate, and do whatever else we can to develop safety and stability in our lives. We use defense mechanisms, addictions, people-pleasing, isolating, etc., to control our feelings and the world around us. And that can work until multiple stressors hit and our seemingly well-constructed psyches crumble. Starting with Step 3, we begin the brutal but liberating process of rebuilding our selves—this time on a stronger, more reliable foundation.

Why Does It Have To Be a Higher Power?

Step 3 asks us to turn our will over to a Higher Power (however it is that we choose to conceptualize and understand that Higher Power). With this act, there is an unspoken understanding that this Higher Power will be a source of love, forgiveness, and grace.

It's my personal opinion that you should never turn your will and life over to anything other than a source like that. If your relationship with a Higher Power only creates more shame, judgment, punishment, and arbitrary rules to follow, you should find another Higher Power. A judgmental, punishing God is not the kind of source that will provide you with liberation from the insanity of worldly control. Love has to be love. It cannot be filled with duty, obligation, requirement, or martyrdom. That's just another form of control and manipulation.

Implementing Step 3

There are many complicated and counterintuitive concepts in Step 3, and they are all important to explore. In this chapter and my discussion of Step 2, I have primarily explored what I believe to be the most important of those concepts: relinquishing our need to control others and the world. Only when we surrender this need will we truly be free.

Overcoming life's problems is not about willpower; it's about the power we can gain when we let go of our will. We must accept what is, what was, what will be, ourselves (exactly as we are), and others (exactly as they are).

That said, surrendering to a Higher Power does not mean we lose our voice, our soul, or our existence. Our walk through life still includes healthy boundaries with others and healthy personal growth. That is how we become vulnerable in a healthy way. That is how we relinquish unhealthy attempts at control and welcome the support (and occasional hurt) provided by other people.

That's the vulnerability part of Step 3—the exposure to hurt due to the whims of the world and other people's choices. The answer to our fear of being vulnerable in this way, for better or worse, is not to armor up and avoid connection. The answer is to turn the behavior of other people and the world at large over to a Higher Power, and to focus on the one thing we can control—ourselves. We are in charge of our own thoughts and behaviors; our Higher Power is in charge of the rest. And when we trust that our Higher Power is a loving, caring, forgiving entity, this task of "turning it over" is much easier. It may even be a relief.

Step 3, Exercise 1: The God Circle

If you are struggling to develop your understanding of a loving Higher Power, the exercises Scott suggests for addicts who face a similar struggle can help, so we'll repeat them in a formalized way here. The first of these exercises is to create a God circle.

First, get a large sheet of paper and draw a giant circle on that sheet of paper. Inside the circle, list attributes you want and need from your Higher Power. Probably you will come up with things like loving, caring, honest, funny, protective, and nurturing, plus a few others. You can also clip images from magazines or elsewhere that represent these traits in ways that are meaningful to you, pasting those images in the circle. Then do the same thing with undesirable traits—angry, judgmental, punishing, controlling, and the like—but write those words and paste those images outside the circle.

Next, use a pair of scissors to cut away whatever is outside the circle. These undesirable traits should then be ripped up, ceremonially burned, or disposed of in some other way that makes them fully gone from your God circle.

Finally, take the remaining circle and put it somewhere you will see it several times each day. As you do so, think about your Higher Power as being represented by the traits and images in the circle. If need be, *act as if* this is your understanding of your Higher Power, even if you don't yet believe it. Do this for 30 days, paying attention to how your thoughts about having a Higher Power and turning your will and your life over to that entity's care evolve.

In the space below, write about your experience with this exercise.

____

____

____

Step 3, Exercise 2: Hiring Your Higher Power

Another useful tactic is to write a want ad for your Higher Power. To do this, you should ask yourself three questions.

What do I want from a Higher Power?

____

____

____

How can I learn to trust this Higher Power?

____

____

____

What sort of interactive give and take between me and my Higher Power should occur?

____

____

____

After you've answered these questions, write a brief want ad.

____

____

____

____

____

Once you know what you are looking for with your Higher

Power, you can begin the interview process. Maybe you'll talk to some local religious leaders, maybe you'll take some meditation and yoga classes, maybe you'll share about what you're looking for with friends and loved ones and embark on a spiritual journey together. Write about your experience with this in the space below.

____

____

____

____

____

The good news is that there is no right or wrong when it comes to your Higher Power. If you find a spiritual connection that works *for you*, go with it. And feel free to let your Higher Power evolve as you evolve.

Step 3, Exercise 3: So You're Still Resistant to Having a Higher Power?

Not every person finds a Higher Power at this stage of recovery. Scott admits that his sponsor, after several months of struggle with Step 3, finally asked him to read Step 12. So Scott looked at that step and read, "Having had a spiritual awakening as the result of these steps, we—" At that point, his sponsor cut him off and had him re-read those opening words of Step 12: "Having had a spiritual awakening as the result of these steps, we—" The sponsor then said, "We're going to skip the spiritual version of a Higher Power for now and move ahead with the other steps. In the interim, use your therapist and your 12-Step group as your Higher Power. Then, when we get to Step 12, we'll see if we need to go back to find the spiritual element of Step 3."

Scott laughs about this now and says, "We never had to revisit Step 3. By the time I got to Step 12, I was completely on board with the spiritual nature of Step 3."

So, your inability to find a Higher Power that works for you at this point is not the sticking point that you might think it is. In fact, if you are truly struggling, we ask you to do as Scott did, and simply put the spiritual element of Step 3 on the back burner, as long as you're willing to revisit that later.

If you find yourself struggling at this point to find and connect with a spiritual Higher Power, think about ways you can still find the external guidance and accountability you need. List at least three forms of this "Good Orderly Direction" (words that are often used as an acronym for God) in the space below.

1. ____

2. ____

3. ____

You Can't, God Can, So Let Him

That's the simple sound bite used to summarize Steps 1 through 3. "It's building a stronger foundation of turning your will over to something greater than yourself but also realizing you've been trying to make every other thing in your life your God," said Susan. "I was making my toxic relationship with a narcissistic alcoholic my Higher Power and it was destroying me."

Susan had been in and out of treatment centers dealing with her alcohol abuse and grieving the sudden and untimely death of her husband of 16 years. She would go a few months without alcohol binges only to relapse every time she had a falling out with the man she began dating after her husband died. "I was addicted to him, to our drama, to his lying. He would shower me with love, gifts, and admiration one minute, only to ignore me for days and days, leaving me to feel so hurt and abandoned."

Later, Susan found out her boyfriend had been seeing other women during their entire relationship and would disappear during his own alcoholic binges. "I knew he was unhealthy for me from the very beginning. No one else liked him. Not my family or my friends. But I just could never end it with him."

In retrospect, Susan realized she was using the intensity and drama of their relationship to distract her from her most painful issues: the abandonment and fear she'd experienced when her husband died three years before. Her grief and pain were so powerful and fear-provoking that she found herself running back to a man who psychologically abused her and, ironically, kept her in a state of fear and abandonment. "I would seek him out instead of trusting in a Higher Power to help me through this deep dark pain. In retrospect, it's crazy to think that I preferred to expose myself to that level of abuse and neglect in lieu of trusting in myself and my Higher Power's ability to get me through the most challenging time of my life."

Once Susan cut ties with the man she was dating and endured several months of withdrawal and grief, she began to heal and seek healthier relationships with her family, friends, romantic partners, and herself.

Step 4 for Addicts

Made a searching and fearless moral inventory of ourselves.

Most active addicts consider themselves to be victims, and they use that stance as justification for drinking, using, and engaging in compulsive/addictive behaviors. To this end, addicts say things (to themselves and others) like:

- Nobody understands me. That's why I drink and use and gamble online.
- My boss hates me. I think I'll get even by showing up high.
- My wife is a nag, so why should I go home after work? The women at the bar are more fun.

This list of excuses could continue *ad infinitum*, and often does. Step 4, however, puts a stop to this sort of misguided, maladaptive, "stinking thinking."

With Step 4, addicts take a hard, unrelenting look at their lives. At the end of Step 4, addicts (hopefully) realize that they are not victims; rather, they are active participants in the mess their lives have become. For this reason, many people with long-term sobriety point to Step 4 as the turning point in their recovery.

Before working Step 4, addicts are still battling all of the perceived "problems" in their lives—the *reasons* they have for drinking, using, and engaging in other addictive behaviors. And these reasons are nearly always external—other people, organizations, and occurrences. After working Step 4, addicts know differently.

They understand that the problems in their lives belong to them and no one else.

For me, Step 4 is when I realized that *you* weren't my problem. I was. And once I finally understood that my problem was internal, not external, I was willing to change my thinking and my behavior. As soon as I stopped blaming everyone else and started looking at myself, my life started to get better.

Step 4 is when I realized that *you* weren't my problem. I was. And once I finally understood that my problem was internal, not external, I was willing to change my thinking and my behavior.

Interestingly, there is a tremendous lack of consensus as to the best way to work this cornerstone step. All methods, however, are constructed with the same basic goal in mind: for addicts to see how they have been an *active participant* in their addiction and messed-up life. One of the most commonly used methodologies is outlined below.

List the ways in which you have avoided taking personal responsibility. This may include: blaming others for the problems in your life; using the actions of others as justification for your own bad behavior; lying or keeping secrets to avoid taking blame for something you actually did; and behaving in ways that distract or divert attention from your bad behavior. Be both specific and general, and list as many items as you can.

Examples:

- I told my parents that the drugs in my bedroom belonged to a friend, not me, when they really were mine.
- I told my wife she was being paranoid, that I really did fall asleep on the couch at work, but really, I was out all night

doing cocaine and having sex with a prostitute.

List the ways in which you have misused your anger. This may include lashing out when you were caught in your addiction, using anger to justify your addiction, and nursing grudges and resentments. Be both specific and general, and list as many items as you can.

Examples:

- I am still angry about the way my high school baseball coach treated me. Every time I watch baseball on TV, I feel like drinking.
- I yelled at my kids for making a mess to hide from my husband the fact that I was binge-eating all day.

List the ways in which you have been paralyzed by fear. When did you fail to act even though you should have? What conversations or actions have you put off because you were too afraid to move forward? Be both specific and general, and list as many items as you can.

Examples:

- I have hated my job for years, but I'm too afraid to quit. So instead, I just secretly drink all day to dull the pain.
- I knew that my husband was cheating on me, but I was afraid that if I confronted him, he would leave me. So I just sat quietly and ate prescription painkillers like candy.

List the things you've done that you're ashamed of. Include all instances where you did not live up to your own values or practice what you preached. A good place to start is listing all the things you're keeping a secret. Be both specific and general, and list as many items as you can.

Examples:

- I left my sleeping child alone in the car while I had sex with my affair partner.

- I gambled away my child's college fund.

Yes, that's a pretty rough road to travel, as addicts must to fess up to a lot of lies, fears, and bad behavior. And, amazingly, the process is not over. Now addicts must go back and look at each item on these lists, asking:

- Where was I to blame?
- What was I thinking and feeling?
- What is my part in this?

Another common approach to Step 4 is for addicts to list their resentments, fears, and sexual conduct that may have hurt others.

Resentments tend to fall into a few general categories—family, relationships, work, school, religion, and politics. It is generally suggested that addicts first list every person and institution against whom they have a resentment. Then they write down the nature of the resentment and what part of their self (self-esteem, pride, emotional security, finances, ambitions, personal relationships, sex relationships, physical health, etc.) was hurt or threatened. Finally, they list "their part" in the resentment. Were they dishonest, selfish, self-seeking, angry, inconsiderate, etc.?

After the resentments list is done, addicts move on to fears. Fears can be directed at people, places, events, institutions, and all sorts of other things. To begin, addicts simply list their fears. Once they've created an exhaustive list of fears, they note which aspects of their life (self-esteem, pride, emotional security, finances, ambitions, personal relationships, sex relationships, physical health, etc.) feel threatened by that particular fear. Then they examine how realistic that fear is, and what they might do to stop that fear from controlling their behavior in negative ways (like engaging in addiction as a way to numb out and not feel their fear).

Next, addicts create a sexual inventory. First, they ask, "Whom did I hurt with my sexual conduct?" Then they list exactly what they did to harm that person, paying attention to whether and how their behavior may have aroused jealousy, suspicion, or bitterness. Then, as with resentments, they examine "their part" in the situation, noting where they were selfish, dishonest, inconsiderate, etc.

Once the Step 4 process is complete, regardless of the methodology used to work it, it becomes very difficult for addicts to continue blaming others for their actions. As I sometimes share in 12-Step meetings, Step 4 is when I learned that the asshole in my life was me, not you.

At the end of the day, the goal of Step 4 is for addicts to take a hard, unrelenting look at their problems and their role in creating those problems. After working Step 4, addicts hopefully realize that they are not victims; instead, they are active participants in the mess their lives have become. And believe it or not, this realization is *empowering*. In fact, as stated above, many addicts point to Step 4 as the turning point in their recovery. Before working Step 4, they were battling external factors—other people, events, and organizations that "drove them" to addiction. After working Step 4, they understand that the real enemy lives within, and they, not others, are the cause of their misery, so their addiction belongs to them and no one else.

Step 4 for Non-Addicts

Made a searching and fearless moral inventory of ourselves.

I have always struggled with hearing criticism from others. Personal and professional feedback from others instinctively causes me to become highly defensive, to apologize disingenuously, or to explain my well-thought-out justifications for my behaviors and choices. My natural responses rarely include humbling myself, processing the feedback given, or vetting the feedback for pieces that might be valid or constructive to me. And until recently, criticism from others *never* led me to a searching and fearless moral inventory of myself.

To be perfectly honest, the concept of Step 4 sounded both unnecessary and undesirable to me. My ego was too fragile to handle any person—let alone me—pointing out a chink in my armor, a flaw in my character, proof that I was imperfect or (even worse) unlikeable. When others would share their observations of me, disagree with me, or challenge my choices and perspective, I could barely hear what they were saying. Instead, I heard that I was bad, wrong, defective, and less-than—things I'd worked my entire life to not be. My physical and mental state became overloaded from the shame of my imperfections, and then I would armor-up as a defense. It became a vicious cycle.

After a great deal of internal work, I now understand the opportunities for growth that I had previously missed. Only retrospectively did I realize the importance of exploring all the facets of myself that make up *me*. My good and bad, light and dark. My shame, trauma, and pain. Where I'd been harmed and how I might have harmed others. The not-so-great aspects of my personality (rage, resentment, passive-aggression, entitlement). I also needed to explore and validate my strengths and positive qualities (intelligence, generosity, spirituality, empathy).

Step 4: The Need for Guidance

Your defense mechanisms will get in the way of exploring these difficult topics. That's why this work is meant to be done with a 12-Step sponsor or therapist. Someone to call you out, to help you see what might be initially too painful to acknowledge.

Despite my resistance to constructive criticism, I desperately needed to work Step 4. I needed to make a searching and fearless moral inventory of myself. I needed this inventory to be searching, to leave no crevice of my history, choices, behaviors, emotions, or personality unexplored. I needed it to be fearless because it had to be done without fear of rejection, judgment, or shame (the things that led me to need Step 4 in the first place).

At the end of the day, Step 4 is a humbling process that creates a healthy, reality-based foundation on which to build a more authentic, conscious, resilient person. It also develops a weapon against our archnemeses: fear and shame (unavoidable human affects and experiences that come from the deeply rooted belief that we're not valuable, loved, or worthy of connection with others).

Understanding Shame

Shame is the extremely uncomfortable feeling we get when we've been rejected, hurt by others, or feel like we might not be worthy of or valued by others. Can you identify where you feel shame in your body? What does it feel like? Can you identify when you are most likely to feel shame? Does it always come to you from an external source, or have you learned to create it all by yourself?

Developing a list of ways in which we may be flawed or fall short is not meant to rub our faces in the mud and make us feel worse about ourselves. It's meant to humble our souls and envelop us in the truth and realistic understanding that we're imperfect. This is what humility is: an acceptance of our own reality. Becoming humble in this way is the beginning phase of creating transparency instead of lies, façades, and manipulation. It's admitting to blind spots and personality flaws while letting go of perfection. It's exposing and exploring childhood wounds, painful conflicts, relationship difficulties, moral failures, and poor decision-making.

The goal of Step 4 is not the perfect avoidance of sins, flaws, wrong choices, and mistakes. Because that's not even possible. Step 4 is simply meant to acknowledge and own the struggle of trying to achieve growth, failing miserably at it, and, in conjunction with Step 5, achieving some amount of wisdom and camaraderie as a result. It's also a commitment to the practice of being the best person we can be, regardless of the conditions in which we were raised and the bad choices we may have made.

The ultimate goal of Step 4 for non-addicts is shame resiliency—the freedom and liberation that we experience when we see our entire selves for who we really are. As we engage in this lifelong practice of exploring and owning our good and bad, it creates a sense of relief, of courage, and perhaps even liberation and confidence in being perfectly imperfect.

Step 4 often takes a bit of time to complete. The following are common pitfalls and struggles that non-addicts sometimes face when beginning their work on Step 4.

- **Attempting to complete the step without help from a 12-Step sponsor, professional, or supportive community.** We all have highly adaptive defense mechanisms created to avoid diving into such difficult topics. As such, we need others around us to set the example, help us feel safe, and continue to challenge us to dig deep in this process.
- **Focusing too much on how we were harmed and not enough on how we've harmed others.** Richard Rohr wisely says, "Pain that is not transformed is transmitted." In other words, if we don't take the time to properly assess the pain and wounds we carry, we will inadvertently discharge that pain and hurt onto others. We like to believe that conditions outside ourselves have been the cause of our struggles, rather than our shame, fear, and shortcomings. Sometimes that's true. But just as often, we are also to blame. We are relational creatures that are impacted by others' choices and behaviors. But they are impacted by our choices and behaviors, too.
- **Asserting that "My life isn't that bad. I don't have anything to look at with Step 4."** We don't have to demonize our childhood or our loved ones to complete Step 4. But we do need to acknowledge the contradictions, conflicts, inconsistencies, and incongruencies we've faced. Steps 1 through 3 suggest that all there must be is proof that we've been struggling, that we've tried and our best efforts have left us stuck, and we need to surrender our controlling ways to a Higher Power and other helpful, experienced others. Step 4 is an integral part of that process.

Step 4, Exercise 1: Working Step 4

In his explanation of Step 4 for addicts, Scott discusses two possible ways to work the step. His personal preference (the way he approaches the step with himself and the recovering addicts he works with) is for addicts to:

- List the ways in which they've avoided taking responsibility for their life and actions (including lies and secrets).
- List the ways in which they've misused their anger.
- List the ways in which they've been paralyzed by fear.
- List the things they've done that they're ashamed of.

Then, for each item listed, addicts look at what they were thinking, where they were to blame, and what "their part" was in the situation.

We believe that is an excellent way for addicts to work Step 4. For non-addicts, however, we prefer Scott's alternative way of working the step. It tends to feel like a more palatable approach for non-addicts. It also tends to uncover the real issues that need to be addressed. So the second method of working Step 4, focusing on resentments and fears (and, if necessary, sexual conduct), is what we suggest here.

To begin, create a list of your resentments. Make this list as comprehensive as you can. Consider resentments against family, your partner, your friends, work, school, religion, politics, and whatever else you can think of.

After you've listed the people, places, institutions, and events against whom you have a resentment, list the specific nature of each resentment. Then add a statement about which parts of your life were impacted. As you do this, consider your self-esteem, pride, emotional security, finances, ambitions, personal relationships, sex relationships, physical health, and whatever else you can think of.

Finally, write about your part in the resentment. Were you dishonest, selfish, self-seeking, angry, inconsiderate? Did any part of your behavior make the situation worse? Is there anything you could have done but chose not to do (for whatever reason) that, if you had taken that action, might have made the situation better?

Now make a list of your fears. Make this list as comprehensive as you can. Then, for each fear, note which aspects of your life (self-esteem, pride, emotional security, finances, ambitions, personal relationships, sex relationships, physical health, etc.) feel threatened by that particular fear. Then think about and write about this fear. How realistic is it? How does this fear negatively impact your decision-making and life? What can you do to stop this fear from controlling your behavior in ways that do not serve you or the people you care about?

If sex and relationship issues are part of what led you into the process of recovery—even if those issues were primarily created by someone else (such as a cheating spouse or partner)—we ask that you also create a sexual inventory. This starts with two questions:

1. Who has hurt me with their sexual conduct?
2. Who have I hurt with my sexual conduct?

Then list exactly what harm was done and how that harm occurred. And remember, sex can be used as a weapon, a way to manipulate, a way to control. (This includes withholding or threatening to withhold sex.) Finally, as you did with resentments, write about "your part" in the situation, noting where you were selfish, dishonest, inconsiderate, complicit, fearful, etc.

After completing your Step 4 inventories (resentments, fears, and, if need be, sexual behavior), read through them, paying particular attention to your part in these issues.

Now write a paragraph or two (but no more than that) about what this experience felt like and what you learned about yourself and your place in the world.

Step 4, Exercise 2: Trauma

Generally speaking, trauma (victimization and abuse) is defined as any event or experience (including witnessing) that is physically and/or psychologically overwhelming in the moment or later (when the event is remembered). Trauma is highly subjective, meaning incidents that are highly traumatic to one person might not be traumatic for another.

Trauma typically occurs in one or more of the following forms:

- **Threatening Behavior:** Any action or spoken threat to hurt another person physically, psychologically, emotionally, or sexually.
- **Psychological Abuse:** Emotional abuse (mind games, gaslighting) intended to cause fear and/or confusion in the victim.
- **Physical Abuse:** Any forceful or violent physical action designed to intimidate or to make another person do something against his or her will.
- **Sexual Abuse:** Any non-consenting sexual act or behavior, including behaviors "consented to" by minors, adults who are inebriated, and mentally handicapped people.

People who were traumatized (victimized and abused) as children are at high risk for dysfunctional thinking and behavior in their adult lives. As you work the steps of recovery, it can be very helpful to unravel strands of your trauma history, looking at the ways in which you were victimized and abused, and also the ways in which you may have victimized and abused others.

List important instances in your life in which you may have been abused/victimized. Briefly note your age, the category of abuse, the perpetrator, and how it occurred. Example: Age 11 to 15. Physical abuse. My older brother. He would hit me when nobody else was around.

List important instances in your life in which you feel that you may have victimized others. Briefly note the category of abuse, your victim, and what you did. Example: Psychological abuse. My husband. After he cheated, I blamed every problem in our lives on him.

Do you see any connections between your history of being traumatized and your history of hurting others? If so, describe those links.

Step 4, Exercise 3: Guilt, Shame, Core Beliefs

Guilt and shame are not the same thing. Guilt is a healthy and necessary sense that you have violated your moral code, values, and standards, or that you have stepped on someone else's rights. Shame is a sense of being a failure as a person, of not being good enough, of feeling doubt about yourself at your very core. When you feel shame, you feel as if there is something fundamentally wrong with you as a person.

Examples of Guilt:

- I made a mistake.
- I did a bad thing.
- My behavior was hurtful.

Examples of Shame:

- I am a mistake.
- I am a bad person.
- I am defective and unlovable.

Guilt is a healthy human emotion that tells us we have done something wrong and we need to correct or amend our behavior. Shame, on the other hand, is an internal feeling of "badness" that consistently flares up. Shame leads to a distorted self-image—negative beliefs that inaccurately color the way we see ourselves and the world.

Sadly, most of us, especially if we're new to the process of 12-Step healing, feel shame more often than guilt, with shame creating a distorted and mostly negative self-image. The good news is that once we begin to understand that we are good people who are imperfect, rather than bad people who innately do bad things, our process of healing can truly begin.

List ten things you feel shame about. Example: When I found out my husband was cheating on me, I immediately thought there must be something wrong with me.

1. ______________________________
2. ______________________________
3. ______________________________
4. ______________________________
5. ______________________________
6. ______________________________
7. ______________________________
8. ______________________________
9. ______________________________
10. ______________________________

Pick the three most shameful (emotionally painful) items from list above. For each of these, describe how shame has distorted your self-image, and then list three contrary affirmations.

Example:

- Shame—I gave my wife an STD, and then I accused her of cheating on me.
- Distorted Self-Image—I am a bad person, and I don't deserve to be loved.
- Contrary Affirmations—I am not defined by the mistakes I have made; I can love myself and accept my past; I am recovering with the help and love of others.

Shame: ______________________________

Distorted Self-Image: ______________________________

Contrary Affirmation: ______________________________

Contrary Affirmation: ______________________________

Contrary Affirmation________________________________

Shame____

Distorted Self-Image: _______________________________

Contrary Affirmation: ______________________________

Contrary Affirmation: ______________________________

Contrary Affirmation: ______________________________

Shame: ____

Distorted Self-Image: _______________________________

Contrary Affirmation: ______________________________

Contrary Affirmation: ______________________________

Contrary Affirmation: ______________________________

Now fact-check your distorted self-image with your therapist, your 12-Step sponsor (if you have one), and your close friends. Are these negative core beliefs grounded in reality? Do they match how others see you? How does it feel to hear others tell you your deepest shame is not true?

____

____

____

____

____

Shit Dipped in Gold is Still Shit

To the outside observer, Brent had it all: a beautiful, supportive wife, two kids, friends and family, and a successful business. He also felt that he had a close relationship with God and no problem connecting with others. "I don't have a vulnerability or intimacy issue," Brent said, "I'm honest and open with everyone." His wife quickly replied, "Yes. You're also cutthroat in the way you share your truth, and you're not very good at *accepting* vulnerable or intimate gestures from other people."

Eventually, Brent shared in therapy that he was struggling with feelings of restlessness, perfectionism, and anxiety that were negatively impacting his mental health and relationships. He had occasional bouts of substance abuse, was quick to anger, and often preferred to spend more time mentoring his employees than connecting with his children.

Brent's story is more common than one might think. Countless people appear to have it all together on the outside but struggle internally with contentment, defensiveness, or shame resiliency. They appear to be great with connection in areas of their life where they feel in control or capable, such as their workplace or with casual friends, but they struggle in more intimate settings such as with their loved ones or people they rely on.

"Shit dipped in gold is still shit" is a metaphor that is sometimes used to help people realize that you don't have to be experiencing all the classic, extreme symptoms of substance abuse, suicidal levels of depression, or multiple toxic relationships to realize you need to make changes in your life. On the outside you can appear to have it all, but still deeply struggle inside.

Brent's constant need to perform at his job, make big decisions, and seek out intensity with his substance use or competitiveness wasn't going to kill him or destroy his marriage (at least not in the short-term). But at 42 years old, he was starting to realize that it was an exhausting way of life and it wasn't working for him anymore. He needed to get honest with himself about what he was running away from and trying to out-perform.

When Brent finally worked his Step 4, he uncovered deeply shaming wounds related to undiagnosed dyslexia and being told by teachers that he would never amount to anything as an adult.

These subconscious traumas, resentments, and shame all quietly contributed to Brent's less-than-optimal behaviors and choices. More importantly, they were obstacles to experiencing real connection and real intimacy with those he loved the most. Step 4 helped him see this and provided a path toward recovery and change.

Step 5 for Addicts

Admitted to God, to ourselves, and to another human being the exact nature of our wrongs.

In Step 4, addicts compile an inventory of their wrongdoings, character defects, weaknesses, fears, and just plain crazy behavior. Having done this, they may be feeling more alone than ever—riddled with guilt, shame, and remorse, and completely convinced they are the worst person ever. If this is the case, and it is for most addicts, the thought of working Step 5 by sharing Step 4 with another human being can be downright frightening. Nevertheless, most recovering addicts find that they cannot successfully maintain sobriety while continuing to live a double life filled with secrets and shame.

Not surprisingly, a lot of addicts tell themselves, after completing Step 4, that their most distressing and disturbing memories and behaviors should not be shared and should probably be taken to the grave. Many addicts embark on Step 5 fully intending to leave certain things out. This is not only unwise, it is downright dangerous. Continuing to compartmentalize and hide from others the worst of oneself creates anxiety, depression, remorse, and more—the very emotions that drive people toward addiction in the first place.

The answer to this, of course, is to properly work Step 5, holding nothing back.

The practice of admitting one's character defects and bad

behaviors is ancient, present from the beginning of time in almost every form of religion. That said, religion is hardly the sole advocate of this spirit-saving action. Everyone from ancient philosophers to modern-day therapists has argued for the need to develop meaningful insight into one's personality flaws—insight that can only truly be gained through open, honest, and complete revelation with an understanding, trustworthy, nonjudgmental person.

For addicts, selecting the person with whom they will share their Step 4 inventories is the start of working Step 5. As they undertake that task, they must remember that they will be sharing things about themselves that should probably not become public knowledge, so the person they choose should be someone they trust. Ultimately, most addicts decide to work Step 5 with their 12-Step sponsor. This makes a lot of sense, as their sponsor is the person most directly involved in their quest for long-term sobriety. If, however, they don't feel comfortable working Step 5 with their sponsor (or they don't have a sponsor), a clergy member, a therapist, or even a trusted friend will do.

After that, the process is simple. The addict simply shares his or her Step 4 inventories with that other person, holding back nothing. Sometimes the listener will ask questions or point out patterns of behavior that he or she sees. Other times, that individual will just sit quietly and listen. Occasionally, the person will interject with an admission of his or her own; typically, this is to tell the addict that the listener has engaged in similarly reprehensible activities.

Most recovering addicts say that as they work Step 5, a sense of relief sets in. Grudges, resentments, fears, and toxic shame that have lingered and contaminated their soul for years miraculously vanish as soon as the underlying events are exposed. And the fact that the person who just heard the worst of their secrets will still talk to them afterward—well, that's just icing on the cake. In this way, Step 5 is where the terrible isolation of active addiction finally starts to lift. After working it, addicts no longer feel as if they are alone in the world.

Though Step 5 is one of the simplest steps to work, most addicts approach it with dread. And that is a perfectly understandable feeling to have given the nature of what they're about to do—sharing their Step 4 inventories with another person. But no matter how much addicts dread the prospect of Step 5, they must work it, because they cannot and will not progress in their recovery while keeping shameful secrets.

Step 5 for Non-Addicts

Admitted to God, to ourselves, and to another human being the exact nature of our wrongs.

Every aspect of the 12-Step model creates a dynamic and challenging journey of self-discovery and positive change, and Step 5 is no exception. Steps 1 through 3 ask us to rigorously explore and identify what, exactly, we're struggling with, to humble ourselves with the realization that we cannot solve our problems alone, and to perform the most vulnerable act of all—to surrender our will and lives to a Higher Power (to accept that we are not the ones in control in this uncertain world). Step 4 continues this arduous process by asking us to examine every facet of our lives and personalities, especially the parts we truly don't want to look at or revisit, and then to create a searching and fearless inventory of our wounds, strengths, scars, failures, and successes.

After all of that exhausting and painful exploration occurs, Step 5 commences the healing process. And the healing starts by admitting (or confessing, if you prefer that word) all that we've learned from the previous four steps to our Higher Power and a supportive team around us.

Shame Resiliency: Created By Telling Your Story

It's a brutal process to identify all the ways we've been harmed, all the ways in which we're capable of harming others, and all the shame we carry around. It's not the sort of stuff we want to share. Yet the worst thing we can do after all that soul-searching is to keep it to ourselves. Shame—otherwise known as the intensely painful, unconscious belief that we're "not enough" and we don't deserve to be loved—festers in the dark depths of our brains. But, as Dr. Brené Brown notes after years of researching shame and shame resiliency, if we share our story with someone who responds with empathy and understanding, shame cannot survive. Shame thrives in darkness; it withers in sunlight.

After digging up all the darkness that surfaces from Steps 1 through 4, it's imperative that we bring this information to the light. It's even more important that we share it with people who can welcome our darkness with compassion and without judgment. Speaking our shame to a safe, supportive group and a Higher Power does a number of important things to ignite healing and change. These changes are discussed below.

After digging up all the darkness that surfaces from Steps 1 through 4, it's imperative that we bring this information to the light.

First and foremost, Step 5 is about more than just acknowledging our pain, trauma, and shame. There's an accountability component that comes with admitting our struggles and problems to a Higher Power and other humans. When shameful secrets are dancing around in our heads, we can deny, minimize, distract from, and change our history and reality. When we speak our truth to others, it makes our truth more real, more concrete. Sharing our shameful secrets with others pushes those secrets out of our minds and into the light, where we can see them, fully acknowledge them, and deal with them in a healthy way.

Clarity and perspective are gained when we speak our story to others. Of course, sharing our flaws, pain, and trauma may at first feel extremely shaming—like obvious evidence of our unrelenting deficiencies. But sharing our story with others who *empathize with and understand the struggle* overcomes this. Our perspectives and experiences can feel very different when they're sitting unchallenged or unprocessed in the back of our brain versus when they are shared with empathetic, understanding others.

Who Should Hear Your Step 5?

Addicts, by nature, are prone to lying, manipulating, and minimizing their thoughts and behaviors. As a consequence, addicts are mentored by those who have struggled in similar ways and have walked the path of recovery. Those mentors are called sponsors. Sponsors have worked the steps and understand the steps. Sponsors can also see through an addict's lies and deceits because they've told most of the same lies themselves at some point. This is one of the primary reasons an addict's sponsor is the best person to hear the addict's fifth step. To state it crassly: You can't bullshit a bullshitter.

Non-addicts can seek similar assistance from a variety of options. Most notably, they can join a 12-Step program for non-addicts like Prodependence Anonymous or Al-Anon and find a sponsor in that program, just as an addict would find a sponsor in AA or some other addiction-focused program. Support groups and friends in recovery can also be quite helpful. As stated earlier, I learned a lot about the 12 Steps from co-workers and clients in recovery who shared their journeys with me. Mental health professionals with experience and training in addiction recovery might also be helpful.

A bit of advice when attending 12-Step meetings: While many members have experienced great personal growth, established stability, and are now ready, willing, and able to help newer members like yourself, there are also members who are still in a state of pain, hurt, and incongruency. In short, the people you meet in 12-Step meetings will be a mixed batch. With Step 5, you'll want to look for people who have what you want in terms of serenity and mastery of the steps. You also want to look for people who will understand and express empathy for your pain.

You may have noticed my use of the words "empathetic" and "understanding" when describing who should hear our Step 5. That is intentional. The person or people with whom we choose to share our painful secrets is important. Choosing the wrong confidante can lead us deeper into shame, rather than out of it. The Alcoholics Anonymous book, *Twelve Steps and Twelve Traditions*, best explains the role of those who bear witness to our Step 5:

> *They comfort the melancholy one by first showing us that our case is not strange or different, that our character defects are probably not more numerous or worse than those of anyone else in AA. This the listener promptly proves by talking freely and easily, and without exhibitionism, about his or her own defects, past and present. This calm yet realistic stocktaking is immensely reassuring.*

A natural response to acknowledging our shortcomings and trauma is to become caught in a shame spiral of feeling we're less-than, broken, and unworthy. Shame spirals lead to unhealthy coping skills and disconnection from others. Shame sparks pain and suffering, not healing. Shame drives addiction, manipulative behaviors, mental and emotional struggles, and general unhappiness. But admitting our flaws to empathetic others can start us down a path toward understanding, acceptance, and shame resiliency. In this way, Step 5 is a vital step in self-discovery and the healing process. In fact, when shame is brought into the light, we often find that we've been yearning to be fully seen and accepted by others *and ourselves* for a very long time.

Admitting our flaws to empathetic others can start us down a path toward understanding, acceptance, and shame resiliency.

Our trauma, shame, and flaws sit in the back of our brain in the fight/flight/freeze region. This is the "lizard brain" that was wired eons ago for survival and impulsive, caveman-like instincts. (In other words, it is *not* the well-thought-out, complex-minded thinking that occurs in the more evolved parts of our brain). The longer that our trauma, shame, and flaws remain hidden in our lizard brain, unacknowledged and unchallenged, the more likely they are to unconsciously bleed into every behavior we engage in. Working Step 5, speaking our wrongs and our shame to others, helps bring this information to the higher functioning parts of our brain, where rational thought and good judgment can filter our thoughts and actions. Dr. Peter Levine, a trauma expert, explains this in his book, *Waking the Tiger*, writing:

> *Traumatic symptoms are not caused by the "triggering" event itself. They stem from the frozen residue of energy that has not been resolved and discharged; this residue remains trapped in the nervous system where it can wreak havoc on our bodies and spirits. The long-term, alarming, debilitating, and often bizarre symptoms of PTSD [Posttraumatic Stress Disorder] develop when we cannot complete the process of moving in, through and out of the "immobility" or "freezing" state.*

So we share our wrongs with a Higher Power with hopes that this Higher Power (as we understand it) can meet our wrongs with unconditional love and forgiveness. As Richard Rohr asserts in *Breathing Under Water*, "God doesn't love us if we change, God loves us so we can change."

In many ways, Rohr is speaking about the difference between retribution and restoration. For the most part, our society espouses retributive justice over restorative justice. Retributive justice is the idea that when we make a mistake, we are punished, and that response will lead us to want to change and be better. Retributive justice supporters believe that punishing mistakes and wrongdoing (or fearing punishment) is the best tactic to drive the transformation of our soul and choices. Restorative justice is the opposite. It is the idea that when we make mistakes and bad choices and we are loved anyway, we are then moved by grace to transform and change our behavior. Restorative justice is what we find in the 12 Steps. When a Higher Power and others can love and forgive us in spite of and even because of our trespasses, we are then moved by grace to transform and change our behavior.

The practice of sharing our story with a Higher Power and others is the foundation of the 12-Step community. It promotes connection and the desire to be of service to others. We share our stories and we are transformed with the telling. At the same time, others are transformed by hearing it. This also happens when others share their story; they are transformed, and so are we.

When stories are shared in a supportive setting, new neuropathways are developed and we can change the habits that led to our struggles. We and our community can work toward self-love and self-acceptance as we gather and speak the full, authentic truth to one another. Our shame is wiped away as we share the dark debris of our lives, receive support from others, and then return the favor for individuals who are equally imperfect and struggling with their own darkness.

Step 5 may be the most significant step in the process of healing in terms of gaining long-term joy and contentment. Step 5 is also a core step in developing shame resiliency. Step 5 is when we learn that we can identify and face the brutal truth, learning from it and becoming better for it. But it is only when we willingly share our deepest, darkest secrets with supportive, empathetic others that we begin to release our shame, build true connection, and move forward into healing.

Step 5, Exercise 1: Understanding Our Shame and Shame Triggers

This exercise is adapted from material in Dr. Brené Brown's book, *I Thought it Was Just Me (But It Isn't)*.

Shame is an extremely difficult thing to teach and bring into our conscious, everyday awareness. However, the two most effective questions to ask yourself when exploring your potential "shame voices" are:

- I want to be perceived by others as...
- I do not want others to perceive me as...

Below is a list of common areas in your life where you might develop shame. Explore what your thoughts, ideas, and perspectives are toward others and yourself with these topics. Explore the "best" and "worst" scenarios (in your opinion) about these topics. Then explore where the origins of these opinions came from. For instance, regarding appearance and body image, I may value having a certain body type that I deem desirable. I may consider being overweight or not looking "put together" as less-than-ideal. And the origins of these opinions may come from growing up in Southern California, where the culture is focused on being attractive, or from my family, who would often show me that we are more valuable when we are attractive and that being attractive is a way to feel special.

In each category, fill out the first column by asking yourself, "How do I want to be perceived?" Then fill out the second column by asking yourself, "How do I *not* want to be perceived?" Be as specific as possible. Then ask yourself, "What does that mean?" or, "What would that look like?" or, "How would I know I was achieving this or if I was blowing it?" and, "From where did I get this message?" The answers to those questions will help you fill out the final column.

Aspects of Life and Personality	**Ideal/Desired Identities and Characteristics**	**Unwanted Identities and Characteristics**	**Origin of that Perspective/Belief**
Appearance/ Body Image			
Being in a Relationship			
Sex/Sexuality			
Money/ Spending			
Work/Success			
Experiencing/ Expressing Emotion			
Your Family			
Getting Older/Dying			
Religion/ Spirituality			
Substance Use/ Addiction			
Parenting/ Children			
How to Handle Adversity			

Step 5, Exercise 2: Practicing Shame Resiliency

This exercise is adapted from the shame resiliency work of Dr. Brené Brown.

You can't cure shame. As long as you have the desire to want to love and connect with others, you'll have a deep fear of not being "enough" to be loved and wanted. You can only take steps to become more resilient to shame.

To better understand your shame and the process of developing shame resiliency, please answer the following questions.

Recognize Shame

What does shame feel like? ______________________________

____

What does shame look like? ______________________________

____

Where do you feel shame in your body (the physical symptoms)? _

____

What does shame smell like? ______________________________

____

What color is shame? ______________________________

____

Understand What's Triggering the Shame Reaction

What is the story I'm telling myself about what happened? ______

____

____

Did I do something, did someone say something, did I just see or remember something? ___________________________

____

____

What do I think the other person is thinking about what happened? ___________________________________

____

____

Practice Critical Awareness of the Origins of Shame

When we are in shame, we become hyper-focused on our flaws, shortcomings, and pain, and those elements of shame quickly pile on top of each other. Shame always begets more shame. To combat this, we must:

- Know how shame works, stay curious, ask what's happening, what triggered it.
- Explore what parts are shame, guilt, trauma, embarrassment, etc.
- Reality-check our shame, realizing that everyone experiences this to some degree.

To accomplish these tasks, we must understand what triggers our shame.

Where do you find most of your shame triggers come from? ____

____

____

Reach Out to Others

Sharing our story with others who can listen with empathy and non-judgment helps us to realize that shame is a human experience and that we're not alone in the experience.

The act of talking about our shame also brings it to the executive functioning levels in the brain, which is where we practice rational thought, good judgment, and impulse control. The more time and thought we put into the "shame voices," the more we can put those voices through a rational filter instead of always viewing our shame through the "trauma" or "survival" part of our brain.

List some safe people with whom you might feel comfortable sharing your story?

1. ______________________________
2. ______________________________
3. ______________________________
4. ______________________________
5. ______________________________

Working Through the Shame

When we own our story, sharing the shame voices that we're hearing, we take shame's power away.

Write about what it feels like to share "the shame story I'm telling myself."

____

____

____

What are some "down-regulating" skills (breathwork, exercise, meditation, yoga, etc.) that you can use to deal with shame?

____

____

____

Write a statement about what it would be like to practice self-compassion instead of constantly beating yourself up.

____

____

____

Additional Points to Help with Shame Resiliency

- Realize one good deed doesn't cancel out a crappy thing you did. Everything must be acknowledged and processed.
- Make amends whenever necessary or possible. It's never too late.
- Use trauma treatment/healthy coping skills to manage distress, including down-regulation skills.
- Avoid lying or manipulating others so you can "keep your side of the street clean."
- Remind yourself that when you behave in a less-than-ideal way, it's most likely due to trauma, shame, and your defenses. Once you consciously process what went wrong, you need to forgive yourself and do better next time.

Do any of these points resonate with you? If so, which ones, and why?

____

____

I Really Have to Tell You Something

It was Jamie's fifth stint at a treatment center for severe depression and anxiety. During her work on uncovering her trauma history, she came forward with a deep, long-term secret she'd held onto for decades: She'd been sexually abused as a child by a neighbor. She never told a soul, and, as she entered her teen years, the trauma of her early sexual abuse led her down a path of using sex as a currency and a way of seeking power and acceptance. She had sex with many men, some of whom were dangerous and abusive.

Despite being able to share such a sensitive story with her empathetic, non-judgmental support group, she couldn't share it with her most intimate partner: Her husband, Daniel. "I never cheated on my husband," she asserted. "The minute I met Daniel, I straightened out and remained monogamous. But I always felt like he should have known all the bad things I did before we met."

Jamie felt immense shame and unworthiness from her abuse and sexual acting out. She wanted love and acceptance from her husband but felt like if he really knew all the shameful, humiliating experiences she went through, he wouldn't really love her. So her secrets were an obstacle to feeling truly loved and seen by her husband.

Jamie explained to her therapist, "I tried to tell him one time during a family session with my previous therapist, but he quickly cut me off, shaking his head, saying he didn't need to know about things that happened before our marriage. That only made it worse. It reinforced the fear I had all along, that he wouldn't really love and accept me if he knew all that had happened to me and all that I had done. I felt like our 24 years of marriage was a sham based on lies."

The secrets about her past continued to eat away at Jamie's self-worth and fed her shame. Her support team helped her work up the courage to finally share her story with her husband in a way that felt safe for both her and her husband. Fortunately, Daniel received her story with understanding and acceptance. He also apologized for not listening when she'd tried to share her story previously.

With this, Jamie felt the deep relief that had been missing for years. She couldn't believe the relief she experienced after sharing her dark secrets and having her husband love her in spite of it all.

Her shame quickly dissipated. She felt closer and more connected to her husband.

Note on Steps 6 and 7

Steps 6 and 7 are, for addicts, separated for a reason. Basically, Step 6 prepares addicts for the task they undertake in Step 7. With Step 6, addicts identify their character flaws and become willing to let go of them. With Step 7, they begin the actual process of letting them go. Because AA and other 12-step recovery programs for addicts present these steps separately, Scott has done the same with his discussion of how addicts work these steps. Kristin, however, has chosen to discuss these steps simultaneously because for non-addicts that has proven to be effective. Basically, we believe that addicts should work these steps separately, usually in quick succession, whereas non-addicts are better off working them as one.

Thus, you will see Scott's writing on Step 6 followed by his writing on Step 7, and then you will see Kristin's writing on how non-addicts can approach the two steps simultaneously. This is a conscious decision on our part, as we think it is the best way to convey the necessary information to differing populations. We hope that no one will take offense at this approach.

Step 6 for Addicts

Were entirely ready to have God remove all these defects of character.

The Alcoholics Anonymous book, *Twelve Steps and Twelve Traditions*, famously calls Step 6 "the step that separates the men from the boys." What the AA folks mean by this is that compiling a list of one's character defects and then becoming completely, absolutely, and totally willing to let go of those defects requires a lot of fortitude, especially when some of those supposed defects are, in moderation, also useful and even necessary elements of life.

The trick here is to realize that these life-sustaining natural instincts (for sexual congress, eating, security, and the like) are good things *until they spiral out of control*. In other words, when these naturally instilled survival instincts begin to drive us blindly into regrettable behaviors, they become character defects. So, if lust is ruining your marriage (because you are routinely cheating on your spouse, for instance), the natural desire for sex has become a character defect that you might like to curtail.

The first part of working Step 6, of course, is figuring out what your character defects are. Having worked Step 4, you probably have a pretty good idea about that already. If not, it is usually very helpful to re-read your Step 4 inventory, looking for patterns of fear, dishonesty, greed, lust, jealousy, grandiosity, willfulness, sideways anger, and the like. As you go along, you can write down each individual character defect you spot.

Once you have compiled your list of character defects, you can write, next to each character defect, a corresponding trait that you'd like to replace it with. For instance, if you identify "lust" as a character defect, you could choose "marital fidelity" as something you aspire to. If "lying" is a character defect, you might choose "honesty and transparency" as things to shoot for. Etc. There is no set number of character defects that you should be trying to identify. Your list will be as long as it needs to be.

At this point, you may be asking, "How do I become *entirely ready* to have God remove these defects?" The answer is that you probably don't. The best you can really hope for is to *try* to become entirely ready. If you make an honest effort in that regard and continue that effort on a regular basis, the process eventually gets easier. But no one has ever worked Step 6 perfectly, and no one ever will. And that is perfectly OK.

For some recovering addicts, it helps to realize that in letting go of their character defects they are not "giving something up." Rather, they are learning to behave differently and in ways that better serve them; they are not losing, they are gaining by acquiring new skills. Compiling a list of affirmations can be useful in this regard. A good exercise for this is taking each character defect and writing three to five positive statements about living differently. These affirmations should be worded as if you've already conquered the defect. For example, with "lying" you might write:

- I am telling the truth in all matters.
- I no longer keep secrets from important people in my life.
- I feel better about myself when I tell the truth than when I am dishonest.

For some recovering addicts, it helps to realize that in letting go of their character defects they are not "giving something up." Rather, they are learning to behave differently and in ways that better serve them; they are not losing, they are gaining by acquiring new skills.

Repeating these affirmations aloud at the start and close of each day is a great way to realize that letting go of character defects really does result in a better life. And that realization inevitably creates much of the willingness needed for Step 6. (Affirmations are also useful with Step 7.)

Step 7 for Addicts

Humbly asked God to remove our shortcomings.

In Step 6, addicts identify their character defects and become willing to live without them. Step 7 is the logical continuation of that effort. Stated simply, with Step 7 addicts begin the process of actually getting rid of their shortcomings. In most respects, working Step 7 is a relatively straightforward procedure. Addicts simply incorporate into their daily routine (prayer, affirmations, or whatever else it is that seems to work for them in their recovery) a request that their Higher Power remove their character defects. If there are shortcomings that are particularly irksome to them at a given time, it is helpful to specifically mention those defects.

Sometimes addicts get hung up on the "God" language of Step 7, thinking their lack of belief will hold them back. This is not in fact the case. As always in 12-Step recovery, a belief in God is not necessary, though many recovering addicts do find a spiritually based Higher Power helpful. If, however, addicts do not have a spiritual Higher Power at this point, they can just state aloud their desire to eliminate their character defects as a mantra. For most addicts, the mere realization that these character defects exist, coupled with the contrary action of saying aloud that they would like to be rid of them, results in significant progress.

It must be noted that asking for one's shortcomings to be removed will not automatically make them go away. It is up to the individual to be aware of his or her shortcomings on an ongoing basis, to pay attention when they crop up, and to quickly self-correct whenever this occurs.

That said, many addicts believe that their Higher Power can and does remove their character shortcomings when asked. The problem, they say, is that their Higher Power will also return those defects, without charge, any time they want to re-engage with them. In this way, Step 7 is a prime example of the much-used 12-Step adage: *progress not perfection*. Sometimes that progress occurs in leaps and bounds; other times it is so incremental as to hardly be noticeable. Either way, the primary goal of Step 7 for addicts is that their character defects will become less of a problem over time.

In many ways, Step 7 is about achieving humility. Humility is a word that is often misunderstood—conflated with the word humiliation, which is nearly always unpleasant to experience. And while humiliation sometimes does lead to humility, that is not necessarily or always the case. Humility is simply seeing the truth of one's life and one's place in the world. It is the art of being "right-sized," neither too big (self-entitled, grandiose, etc.) nor too small (ashamed, unworthy, defective, etc.)

For addicts in recovery, developing a sense of humility (seeing and accepting reality) starts with Step 1. The mere act of admitting that they are powerless over alcohol, drugs, or an addictive behavior is a giant leap toward humility in that the addict, perhaps for the first time, has finally begun to see and admit the reality of his or her addiction—the lack of control, the directly related negative life consequences, etc.

Interestingly, admitting powerlessness and unmanageability—that very first act toward humility—creates in nearly all recovering addicts a strong sense of peace, even if that sensation is only temporary. Working Step 7, a much more comprehensive act toward humility, typically results in an even greater (and longer-lasting) sense of peace. It is at this point that recovering addicts realize that humility is not a condition of groveling despair, but a state of peace, grace, and acceptance of life on life's terms. For people who've heretofore known only depression, anxiety, fear, and secrets, this newfound sense of serenity is a priceless gift. It is also an incredibly powerful motivator for continued sobriety and further step-work.

Steps 6 and 7 for Non-Addicts

Were entirely ready to have God remove all these defects of character.

Humbly asked God to remove our shortcomings.

As we examine Steps 6 and 7, it's important to understand that the path through the 12 Steps is not an arbitrary one. The steps are in a particular order, and that order serves a valuable purpose. Steps 1, 2, and 3 help us identify our problem(s) and lean into the discomfort of owning that we need help from others to fix our issue(s). Step 4 asks us to dig deep and explore all aspects of our lives—our character and every facet of our story, especially parts that may have contributed to our struggles and strife. Then the healing begins with Step 5, when we share our story with a safe group of others and our Higher Power, and we find that our story is met with empathy, compassion, and nonjudgmental acceptance. This provides relief from the shame of our trauma, hurt, and mis-takes. However, the healing impact of Step 5 will be short-lived if we do not follow it with Steps 6 and 7.

Up to this point, we've done a lot of work to put a name to our pain, poor choices, trauma, and shame. Now it's time to stop the insanity by ceasing the unhealthy patterns in which we've engaged. The first five steps we worked helped us realize that sometimes our best intentions and thinking fall short and create, rather than get us out of, our struggles and pain. Thus, we must now humble ourselves and invite a Higher Power to ignite meaningful change.

We cannot engineer this transformation on our own because it will end up being self-centered and flawed, per our usual, courtesy of our many defects of character. Changing based on our own thinking and will would be like an alcoholic defining his own rules for sobriety. (Perhaps something like, "If I don't drink before 5 p.m., I'm OK.") Such actions might work temporarily, but eventually these misguided efforts to control and manipulate will fail, putting us back at Step 1. So we must ask for help with our character defects from a power greater than ourselves. The fact that this process is broken down into two steps highlights two things:

1. Accomplishing this task is incredibly difficult and work-intensive, so we must take it piecemeal.
2. Accomplishing this task is incredibly important, so we must do it purposefully and as completely as possible.

To begin the process, Step 6 asks us to become entirely ready to have our defects of character removed. The fact that this step asks us to become "entirely ready" suggests that our struggle with our various shortcomings will be lengthy. In fact, it is usually a lifelong effort rather than a one-and-done experience. Therefore, we must be patient with the process.

One of my colleagues who got sober in his 20s shared that when he was working with his sponsor, his sponsor had him place all his coffee cups under his bed. My friend went on to explain that he was a petulant young adult who thought he had it all figured out, so his sponsor wanted him to "start every day humbled and on his knees." By needing to reach down under his bed, first thing each day, in pursuit of his morning cup of joe, he was forced to think in ways that fostered the development of humility. Sometimes behavioral adjustments like this can lead to soul changes, altering the ways we think and feel and changing our lives. Whatever works, right?

Once we are entirely ready and willing to let go of our character defects, Step 7 suggests that we "humbly ask" our Higher Power to help us. Sometimes this request takes place in the form of a prayer or meditation. Other times, it's a written or verbal request for help from a power outside ourselves. Whatever our interpretation of Step 7 happens to be, it's a process of humbleness and surrender that allows a Higher Power, in whatever form we envision that entity, to help us with the parts of our lives that need to be changed, altered, or transformed. Step 7 can also be viewed as an act of faith, an act of opening our hearts and minds and letting go of our need/desire to always be in control.

Generally, our Higher Power's process of *removing* our shortcomings is a process of *replacing* them with other, more satisfying traits and ways of being. That way, our character defects aren't controlled or pushed away as much as they are exposed and identified as false programs for happiness. That's the difference between superficial behavioral changes and deeper, more permanent soul changes.

Removing character defects and shortcomings should not be confused with the pursuit of perfection. Addressing character defects is not externally motivated or shame-driven, as we see with perfectionism. The change we're humbly requesting is the pursuit of spiritual and moral excellence that involves the expulsion of thoughts and behaviors that create problems in our lives, such as telling lies, judging others, self-righteous indignation, gluttony, manipulation, etc. These are behaviors that we're all capable of that often feel as if they are external, but that, in reality, are internal and drive our shame.

Removing character defects and shortcomings should not be confused with the pursuit of perfection. Addressing character defects is not externally motivated or shame-driven, as we see with perfectionism.

Every day we stand trial against our shame voices—the voices that are constantly trying to convince us that we are not good enough, not smart enough, not attractive enough, not successful enough, not worthy of love and affection. Steps 6 and 7 help us fight these voices by helping us see who we really are and to make changes accordingly. When our shame voices start to whisper (or scream) in our heads, telling us all the reasons we're not good enough, the personal growth we can achieve from Steps 6 and 7 can shut those voices down.

These two steps can be nuanced and difficult for non-addicts because our shortcomings and flaws can seem so normal and commonplace amongst our culture. We can look across our general population and see lots of examples of people who flirt inappropriately, spend money frivolously, rage at strangers or loved ones, etc. For the most part, we look normal and maybe even successful. But inside we struggle to be still, suffer with "imposter syndrome," and drown in a bottomless pit of discontentment and shame. Most of our counterproductive or incongruent behaviors exist to artificially protect us from all the discomfort, trials, and adversity that we experience internally (and then manifest externally).

In addiction recovery, they call this concept "rock bottom," the metaphorical "aha" moment when an addict's life becomes "bad enough" to want to change it (i.e., a divorce, an arrest, going broke, contracting a serious disease, nearly dying). For non-addicts, life may never become so obviously "bad enough." Everything remains "just OK enough" to continue in our unhappy cycle. Therefore, we must be forthcoming about our struggles to ourselves and others in order to become accountable and avoid a false sense of complacency. Surrounding ourselves with a few trusted loves ones or friends who really know us can often save us from ourselves. They can remind us of what we're capable of being at our best and worst, and what we are working to achieve. In other words, they know us intimately enough to call us on our shit.

Steps 6 and 7 are extremely difficult asks because oftentimes our character defects and shortcomings feel like our best friends, talents, and superpowers. At the very least, they have provided us with armor against the vulnerabilities of life and relationships. However, they have also disguised our authenticity and true self, hindering our connection with our spiritual selves and with others.

For instance, I am a masterful liar. I can weave a believable story to spare myself awkward moments or organic consequences for my decisions and actions. I've even caught myself mindlessly lying about stupid, meaningless stuff. If it was up to me, I would never choose to be honest and accountable *all of the time*. I would choose to be honest when it served me, and to lie when it served me.

For me, consistent honesty is extremely inconvenient and uncomfortable. However, I know that any form of lying or manipulating steers me away from my goal of living authentically, vulnerably, and with accountability for my actions. So, for me, lying is a shortcoming (and superpower) that I must surrender to my Higher Power. I must do this because my default state in difficult and vulnerable moments is to lie. Even white lies that seem harmless on the surface are, for me, harmful because *I know that I lied*. Any time I lie, even with good intentions, I know that I have fallen short of being the best person I can be. And those moments allow my shame voices to become louder, causing me to question my value and worth.

It is only with a constant tenacity and humble state that I stay on track with my character defects and shortcomings. Every day I must work with my Higher Power to keep my side of the street clean and to not give my shame voices any type of evidence that proves I'm unworthy, unlovable, and not good enough.

I want to acknowledge here that Steps 6 and 7 can be especially difficult for those who struggle with spirituality, especially those who've been harmed by religious people or establishments. I'm hoping that this book, especially Scott's and my discussion of Step 3, will help readers understand that there can be a significant difference between religious practices and spiritual connections with a Higher Power. And usually, by the time we've come to the 12 Steps for relief, we have tried everything *of* this world and *in* this world to bring us joy and contentment (relationships, therapy, medication, substances, buying things, achieving things, etc.), and we have still not found the answers we're looking for. So maybe we can find some willingness to look outside of ourselves and outside of our material world for assistance.

Steps 6 and 7, Exercise 1: The Circle Plan

Typically, the process of eliminating character defects begins with a list of goals. A few commonly stated goals are:

- I want to focus on my own behavior, rather than the behavior of others.
- I want to be truthful all the time—to not tell lies or keep secrets.
- I want to be more productive at work and at home, to stop "spinning my wheels."
- I want my insides to match my outsides.
- I want to feel worthwhile, good enough, and worthy of love.

Once your goals are clearly stated, you can move forward with the creation of your personalized plan for eliminating your character defects. For this, we recommend using a "circle plan." Circles plans, originally used in sex addiction recovery, are created to support your goals. To this end, they are broken into three levels: the inner circle, the middle circle, and the outer circle.

The Inner Circle

This is a bottom-line listing of your character defects. Here you list the specific behaviors that are causing problems in your life and that you therefore want (and need) to stop. In other words, your inner circle lists the damaging and troublesome acts that are ruining your life. You may list things like:

- Making excuses for my addicted spouse.
- Lying about my struggles so others, including friends and loved ones, don't see the real me.
- Yelling at my kids when I'm feeling sad or lonely or ashamed as a way to cope with my feelings.

- Compulsive eating to cope with feelings.
- Placing more value on how I look than how I feel.

The Middle Circle

This circle lists warning signs and slippery situations that might lead you back to inner circle behaviors. Here you list the people, places, thoughts, fantasies, events, and experiences that might trigger your character defects. In addition to obvious potential triggers—fighting with my spouse, buying six bags of Oreos, looking up an ex-lover's profile on social media—this list should include things that might indirectly trigger a desire to act out—working long hours, keeping secrets, worrying about finances, etc. You may list things like:

- Skipping therapy and/or a support group meeting.
- Lying (about anything), especially to a loved one.
- Feeling hungry, angry, anxious, lonely, bored, tired, etc.
- Fighting and/or arguing, especially with loved ones and/or authority figures.
- Failing to engage in proper self-care—healthy food, getting enough sleep, exercising, etc.

The Outer Circle

This circle lists healthy behaviors and activities that can and hopefully will lead you toward your life goals. These healthy pleasures and coping skills are what you can turn to as a replacement for character defects. Outer circle activities may be immediate and concrete, such as "working on the house," or long-term and less tangible, such as "redefining my career goals." In all cases, the list should reflect a healthy combination of work, recovery, and play. You might list things like:

- Spend more time with my family, especially my kids.

- Reconnect with old friends.
- Rekindle an old hobby (or develop a new one).
- Get in shape, or at least engage in more physical activities.
- Do volunteer work and become more active in my community.

In the space below, list your goals for recovery—what you want to achieve as you work the 12 Steps.

1. ______________________________
2. ______________________________
3. ______________________________
4. ______________________________
5. ______________________________

Your inner circle lists the bottom-line character defects you want to eliminate. Please list these shortcomings and defects in the space below.

1. ______________________________
2. ______________________________
3. ______________________________
4. ______________________________
5. ______________________________
6. ______________________________
7. ______________________________
8. ______________________________
9. ______________________________
10. ______________________________

Your middle circle lists warning signs and slippery situations that might lead you back to inner circle activities. Please list here the people, places, thoughts, fantasies, events, feelings, and experiences that might directly or indirectly spark your character defects.

1. ______________________________
2. ______________________________
3. ______________________________
4. ______________________________
5. ______________________________
6. ______________________________
7. ______________________________
8. ______________________________
9. ______________________________
10. ______________________________

Your outer circle lists healthy behaviors and coping skills that can lead you toward your short and long-term life goals. Please list here the healthy behaviors you can turn to as a replacement for your character defects.

1. ______________________________
2. ______________________________
3. ______________________________
4. ______________________________
5. ______________________________
6. ______________________________
7. ______________________________
8. ______________________________
9. ______________________________
10. ______________________________

Now, based on your answers above, complete the Circle Plan

diagram on the following page, signing and dating the plan to affirm your commitment to change.

MY CIRCLE PLAN

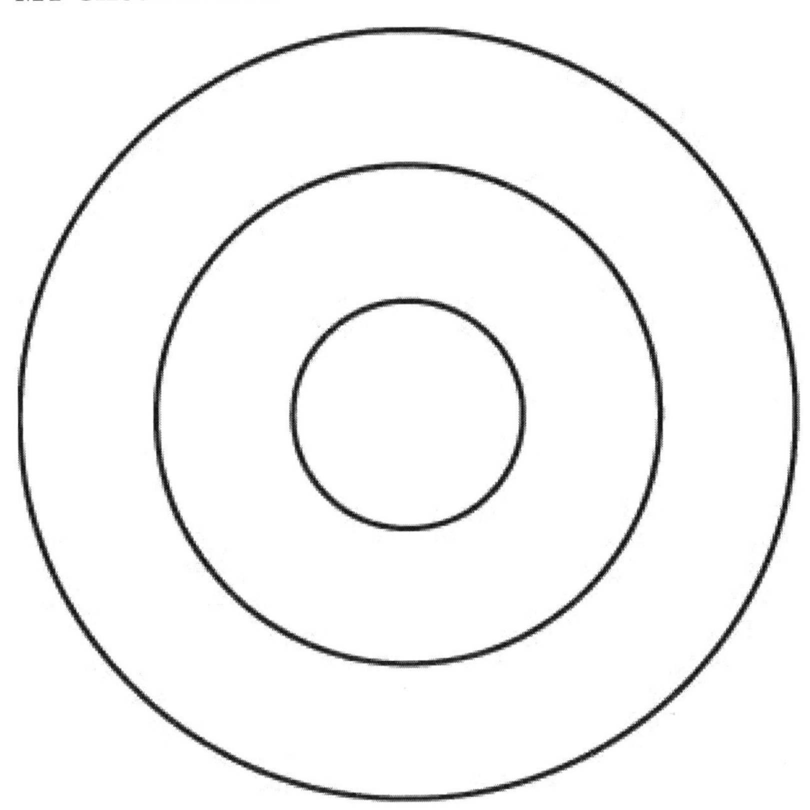

Signature:

Date:

Steps 6 and 7, Exercise 2: Affirmations

One of the most effective ways to combat character defects is to state affirmations to the contrary. Affirmations are powerful messages that confirm your worth, reminding you that who you are today is OK and enough. Affirmations validate that you are not defined by past behaviors, no matter how bad they were. Affirmations are stated aloud daily, often several times per day, as a way to replace your shame-distorted sense of self with self-esteem.

Affirmations are stated positively and in the present tense, as if they are true right now (even though they are, in reality, aspirational). For example, if one of your character defects is lying and keeping secrets, you might create the following affirmations.

- I am rigorously honest in all my affairs.
- I do not keep secrets or tell lies.
- Today, I tell the truth, and I tell it faster.

In the space below, list each of the character defects that appear in your inner circle. Then, for each character defect, create three affirmations.

Character Defect: ______________________________

Affirmation: ______________________________

Affirmation: ______________________________

Affirmation______________________________

Character Defect: ______________________________

Affirmation: ______________________________

Affirmation: ______________________________

Affirmation: ______________________________

Character Defect: ____________________________________

Affirmation: ____________________________________

Affirmation: ____________________________________

Affirmation: ____________________________________

Character Defect: ____________________________________

Affirmation: ____________________________________

Affirmation: ____________________________________

Affirmation: ____________________________________

Character Defect: ____________________________________

Affirmation: ____________________________________

Affirmation: ____________________________________

Affirmation: ____________________________________

Once you have created your list of defects and contrary affirmations, pick the most pressing character defect. Then, each morning and each evening for an entire week, look into a mirror and state aloud your contrary affirmations about that defect. At the end of the week, write about your experience with this in the space below.

____

____

____

Now pick the next character defect on your list and repeat the entire exercise, writing about your experience with each character defect. Continue this process until you've worked your way through your entire list. Know that this is a process you may revisit for the rest of your life, as old behaviors crop up and new character defects are identified.

____

____

____

Looking for Love in All the Wrong Places

Jessica was a 20-something woman who struggled with the idea of being anything other than a feminine, heterosexual female. "My mom would always tell me how excited she was to finally have her "little girl" when she found out she was having me. She dressed me in frilly dresses and wanted to shop and do girl things with me. But all I wanted to do was wear basketball shorts and sports jerseys and roughhouse with my brothers."

When Jessica first entered therapy, she was coming to terms with being attracted to both men and women, while also exploring a non-binary gender identity. The more Jessica embraced the ambiguity of her sexual and gender identities, the more she felt like a disappointment to her family and others. "I'm gay, overweight, a college drop-out, and alone. This is not what my parents wanted."

Whenever her feelings of worthlessness built up to a critical mass, she would seek temporary relief by calling one of her male "friends with benefits" and then she would "let him" have sex with her. "That's easier than being gay," she said.

Over time, Jessica developed a vicious cycle of shame, escapism, abuse, and self-hatred. Eventually, one of her friends in recovery confronted her on her struggle with exploring and owning her sexuality and gender. "My friend says I'm so unhappy because one of my biggest character defects is that I allow unhealthy people to influence me and determine my value and self-worth. Well, that, and I still don't know what my Higher Power is."

Jessica's desperation for the illusion of love and acceptance led her down a path of seeking connection with and approval from anyone who might give it, in lieu of a path toward healthy people who could offer real love and healthy intimacy. Her desperation impeded her ability to practice healthy discernment or boundaries with others. As a consequence, she was surrounded by manipulative and exploitive people who only hurt her more in the end. She also allowed others' expectations and guidelines to define her. What she should look like, what success looks like, what sexuality is acceptable, and what gender looks like were all determined by others instead of Jessica defining them within herself and with her Higher Power.

Ultimately, Jessica's "shortcomings" of allowing others to define her value and worth. Her spirituality issues were the same. As long as she made other flawed humans her god (the source of her value and worth), she was going to struggle in all facets of her life. Finding a spiritual Higher Power allowed her to surrender to her reality and to find peace and acceptance through herself and that Higher Power, instead of looking to other, flawed, human sources to define her sense of self and worth.

Note on Steps 8 and 9

We are taking a similar approach with Steps 8 and 9 as we took with Steps 6 and 7. Scott is writing about these steps separately because that is how addicts should work them. Kristin is writing about these steps simultaneously because that approach seems to work better for non-addicts. Thus, you will see Scott's writing on Step 8 followed by his writing on Step 9, and then you will see Kristin's writing on how non-addicts can approach the two steps simultaneously. Again, this is a conscious decision on our part, as we think it is the best way to convey the necessary information to differing populations, and we sincerely hope that no one will take offense at this approach.

Step 8 for Addicts

Made a list of all persons we had harmed and became willing to make amends to them all.

All of the steps from Step 4 onward are concerned with interpersonal relations—how addicts interact in the wider world, including the pain they've caused (and continue to cause) and what they can do about it. The process, essentially, is:

- Addicts look back on their life and see where they have caused problems for themselves and others.
- Addicts make a vigorous attempt to repair the damage they have done.
- Addicts do what is necessary to live differently in the future.

Step 8, coupled with Step 9, is the middle portion of this procedure—making a vigorous attempt to repair the damage done.

For addicts, the first part of Step 8 is compiling a list of the people they have harmed, not forgetting to include themselves on the list. Reviewing their Step 4 inventory is a great place to start when compiling this list. Most of the names on that list will also appear on the addict's Step 8 list, but some may not, and new ones will likely be added.

Typically, this list includes more than just the injured person's (or institution's) name. Addicts should also write the specifics of the harm done, along with how the aggrieved party reacted to the situation (anger, fear, distrust, depression, etc.) After that, addicts should add their current feelings about the situation, acknowledging emotions like guilt and shame along with any lingering anger or resentments they may have. Next, addicts should examine their motives for making each specific amends. If their goal is simply looking good in the eyes of others, they're probably not yet willing (the second part of Step 8) to make that amends. Finally, they should list the type of amends they can make for each of the harms they've perpetrated.

Addicts should examine their motives for making each specific amends. If their goal is simply looking good in the eyes of others, they're probably not yet willing (the second part of Step 8) to make that amends.

Sometimes the amends can be as simple as admitting what was done, saying "I'm sorry," and not repeating the offense. Other slights may require a financial payment or some other tangible recompense by the addict. It may be that the person the addict has victimized is no longer living or that the situation (theirs or the addict's) is such that further interaction might cause additional damage. In such cases, the best possible amends may be privately vowing to live differently in the future and then actually doing so.

For many recovering addicts, the second half of Step 8—becoming willing to make amends—is more difficult than compiling the list. And when we think about it, this is perfectly natural. The simple truth is most of the people on the addict's list have probably, at some point, behaved badly toward the addict, making it very easy for addicts to seize upon the other person's wrongdoings as a way to excuse their own poor behavior.

If addicts find themselves doing that, they needn't beat themselves up over it. They just need to recognize their feelings and remind themselves that *Step 8 is not about the other person, it's about the addict and his or her recovery.* Addicts are working the 12 Steps, including Steps 8 and 9, for their own recovery, not for the benefit of other people (though others do often benefit).

Recovering addicts sometimes struggle for days, weeks, months, or even years before they find the requisite willingness to make certain amends. When addicts find themselves battling old anger and resentments in this way, they should discuss the issue with their sponsor, therapist, or spiritual advisor. An old 12-Step trick that one of those advisors might suggest is praying (as sincerely as possible) for the other person's health and well-being every morning and night for 30 days. Most addicts find that taking this advice greatly diminishes any lingering resentments.

As with Steps 6 and 7, positive affirmations can be helpful. A few general affirmations that many addicts find useful are:

- I am willing to take responsibility for my actions, regardless of the actions of others.
- I am open to the lessons I can learn from making amends.
- I understand and accept that making amends is a necessary part of my recovery.

More specific affirmations can be even more helpful, such as: "I am no longer angry with X, and I am willing to make amends to him/her for my behavior." Usually, if an addict says this enough times, he or she will start to believe it.

Perhaps the most important thing to know about Step 8 is that this is *not* the point at which the addict actually makes amends. That's Step 9, and Step 9 should *never* be taken until addicts have first discussed their Step 8 list and proposed amends with their sponsor, therapist, or spiritual advisor. Jumping the gun and making amends before the time is right often causes more problems—problems that later require even more amends. So addicts should be patient, making their list and then discussing it before proceeding.

Step 9 for Addicts

Made direct amends to such people whenever possible, except when to do so would injure them or others.

After working Step 8, addicts should have a list of people they have harmed, and they should be willing to make amends to them all. If so, then they are ready to work Step 9. *Step 9 should not be undertaken without the addict first consulting his or her sponsor, therapist, or spiritual advisor.* Period. No exceptions. Addicts must not jump into Step 9 without the assistance and supervision of a mentor who has already worked his or her own Step 9. Jumping the gun on Step 9 is likely to do more harm than good.

In all likelihood, the addict's advisor will ask the addict to discuss his or her Step 8 in detail, asking the addict about his or her goals in making amends, how the addict plans to perform the amends, and when the addict plans to make them. This advisor, having already worked Step 9, understands that timing and prudence are much more valuable to the addict at this point than sheer enthusiasm, and can therefore guide the addict judiciously through the process.

It is important to understand that making direct amends is not always a good idea. That is why the second half of Step 9 reads "except when to do so would injure them or others." It may be that the harm the addict has done to someone is so severe that simply seeing the addict again would cause that person great consternation. In such cases, the addict should probably not attempt a direct amends. It may be that the person the addict has harmed is unaware of the behavior and making them aware will cause them significant pain. Again, a direct amends may not be the best course of action.

It is also possible that approaching someone and admitting bad behavior could stir up the proverbial hornet's nest, putting the addict's job or freedom in jeopardy, which might in turn injure the addict's loved ones—especially if the addict is the family's primary breadwinner. In such cases, direct amends should only be undertaken after much careful consideration by the addict and his or her advisors, plus consultation with anyone else (especially family members) who might be affected. Sometimes an indirect amends—being aware of what was done and working hard to live differently in the future—is the best that an addict can do. If money is involved, donating to a charity the aggrieved party would approve is one way to make an indirect amends.

Most of the time, however, a direct amends can and should be made. In such instances the addict's advisors can help to ensure the addict is making the right amends for the harm done. Sometimes just admitting to bad behavior and saying, "I'm sorry, and I'm working hard to behave differently in the future," is sufficient. Other times, the addict may need to repay, or promise to repay, money that is owed, along with an apology and an assertion that the addict is changing his or her behavior. In all cases, an amends is more than just an apology. The most important part of any amends is the follow-up of not making the same mistake again.

An amends is more than just an apology. The most important part of any amends is the follow-up of not making the same mistake again.

Not surprisingly, Step 9 is among the scariest steps in recovery. And why not? The prospect of approaching people you have wronged, admitting what you've done, apologizing and making restitution when appropriate, and then living differently in the future is, at best, daunting. However, making amends is rarely difficult. Nearly everyone is receptive to a genuinely sincere effort. Sometimes a person that the addict has long held resentments against will use the opportunity to make their own amends to the addict. Usually, at worst, people receiving an amends will appreciate the effort the addict is making toward setting things right.

It is possible, however, that a person to whom an addict attempts to make an amends will not be receptive. This occurs only rarely, but it does sometimes happen. The person may distrust the addict's motives, the person may be so angry with the addict that he or she just can't accept the addict's apology and attempts at restitution, or the person may have an emotional or psychological issue that prevents him or her from behaving as most others do. Such responses are that person's prerogative, and they are not a reason for addicts to deviate from their course. Addicts make their amends anyway. After all, this is the addict's recovery, not the other person's.

For many recovering addicts, Step 9 is a key stride on the road to lasting recovery and a life changed for the better. In fact, this change for the better occurs so often that the book *Alcoholics Anonymous* lists what are commonly called "The Promises" at the conclusion of Step 9. The Promises, as delineated by AA, read as follows:

> If we are painstaking about this phase of our development, we will be amazed before we are halfway through. We are going to know a new freedom and a new happiness. We will not regret the past nor wish to shut the door on it. We will comprehend the word serenity and we will know peace. No matter how far down the scale we have gone, we will see how our experience can benefit others. That feeling of uselessness and self-pity will disappear. We will lose interest in selfish things and gain

> interest in our fellows. Self-seeking will slip away. Our whole attitude and outlook upon life will change. Fear of people and of economic insecurity will leave us. We will intuitively know how to handle situations which used to baffle us. We will suddenly realize that God is doing for us what we could not do for ourselves.

For many addicts, it is helpful and comforting to do a "Promises" check-in after completing Step 9. Nearly always, some or even all the promises have come true, at least to a certain extent. Seeing this tangible proof that the 12 Steps really do work is a great incentive for continued sobriety and step-work.

Steps 8 and 9 for Non-Addicts

Made a list of all persons we had harmed and became willing to make amends to them all.

Made direct amends to such people whenever possible, except when to do so would injure them or others.

In theory, apologizing for harming another person is a sign of maturity and accountability. After all, we are *supposed* to take ownership of our transgressions. We are *supposed* to take appropriate steps to repair the damage we've caused. However, it's important that our attempts to apologize and atone are genuine and are given with full acknowledgment of all the facts and nuances of our transgression.

In my therapy practice, I often see clients or couples who've recently uncovered an extramarital affair. After getting caught, the cheating partner will typically apologize profusely to the betrayed partner, making all sorts of promises and commitments (that are not often kept). The cheating partner might also, interwoven with this apology, minimize or rationalize the harmful behavior and its impact. This type of apology—made from guilt, obligation, and a desire to cool down a crisis—tends to be more counterproductive than helpful.

To be effective, an apology must contain a genuine understanding of what happened, why it occurred, and how it impacted the other person. Until the person who is apologizing is in this frame of mind, any apology that he or she gives will, at best, feel hollow. This is why it's so important for recovering addicts, cheaters, or anyone who's harmed others to avoid making apologies or amends too soon.

Only time and serious contemplation can help these individuals fully comprehend the error of their ways, and to develop the insight they need to avoid making the same mistakes moving forward. That's why the 12 Steps wait until addicts are on Steps 8 and 9 before they even consider the idea of making amends. *Stated very simply, there is a tremendous amount of internal work that must be completed before the addict can begin the process of repairing external relationships by making amends. With apologies and amends, patience really is a virtue.*

Only after the deep, soul-altering, mind-bending work of Steps 1 through 7 are we equipped to own how our choices and experiences have affected others—without minimizing or rationalizing—and work toward repairing unhealthy relationship dynamics.

Merriam-Webster defines making amends as "doing something to correct a mistake that one has made or a bad situation that one has caused." Basically, we do something to show we are sorry for hurting or upsetting someone, especially if what we do makes the situation better for them. So, making amends is an action, not a sentiment.

Amends are birthed from empathy and compassion. They are a product of deep contemplation and authenticity. Amends are without excuses, justifications, or minimization. Amends are not an apology followed by disingenuous promises to correct regretful behavior, nor are they a request for forgiveness. Making amends is a *restorative* act. It is also an opportunity to demonstrate that we have fully explored our actions and choices, examined how they have impacted others, and made the vulnerable and courageous decision to do what we can to repair the damage that has been done.

Too often, we make the critical mistake of attempting to make amends too soon (i.e., before the internal work of Steps 1 through 7 is completed). As stated in Scott's writing on Steps 8 and 9, addicts who try to "skip steps" and apologize without deep contemplation generally end up worse off because their attempts to seek forgiveness and express regret to those they've harmed falls flat. Their attempts at amends are not received as proof of a changed soul. This is because a knee-jerk "I'm sorry, please forgive me" rarely embodies the complexities of a true, fully informed amends.

For non-addicts, Steps 8 and 9 can be more subtle and elusive than they are for a typical addict seeking recovery. Essentially, non-addicts might wonder what they have done that requires amends. After all, they weren't the ones sneaking around, lying about their behaviors, and betraying others' trust. They weren't the ones engaging in *obviously unscrupulous behaviors*. The harm and wrongs that a non-addict may have perpetrated may be much more subtle and difficult to grasp.

Steps 8 and 9 were especially helpful in getting me over a massive hurdle due to my betrayal trauma. I found myself floundering as my relationship ended, and I was desperate to find a healthier way forward. I spent a lot of time talking to a friend who was in recovery about my relationship problems, and he'd always help me by applying the 12-Step principles to my non-addict struggles.

One day, I was in an especially deep vortex of pain, talking about all the ways I'd been wronged and hurt by my estranged partner—the lies, the betrayals, the emotional abuse. I went on and on to my confidant. Finally, he stopped me and asked, "Have you considered your part in all this, Kristin?"

That sentence felt like a gut punch. I gasped with righteous indignation in response to the preposterous suggestion that I might have a role in my seemingly endless relationship woes. So I said, "My part? I didn't ask for this! I didn't want to be lied to or betrayed. I don't deserve any of what happened to me." Then I once again reminded him of all the ways my partner had harmed me.

My friend nodded his head in agreement and said, "Kristin, you're right. You were victimized by the lies and betrayal, and you have every right to be upset about that. But your goal is to heal from this trauma and move forward in a healthier way, right? So maybe you should consider the ways you fell short in the relationship. And maybe you should look at how you've behaved during and after your relationship's unraveling."

I sat with the pain of his words for weeks until finally they began to soften my heart and change my soul.

This exchange and exploration changed my entire outlook on what I was struggling with and healing from. For so long, I'd been paralyzed by my victimhood—more invested in being hurt and angry than in healing and moving on. I was trapped in the powerlessness of my victimhood until my friend gave me the invitation to look beyond how I was harmed and to explore the ways I, too, had perpetrated harm on others (including my spouse).

I was trapped in the powerlessness of my victimhood until my friend gave me the invitation to look beyond how I was harmed and to explore the ways I, too, had perpetrated harm on others.

Exploring ways that I needed to make amends and improve upon my relationship dynamics helped me move from a paralyzed state of pain and suffering to a place of empowerment. From Victim to Victor. From Anger to Empathy. From Shame to Self-Compassion.

I worry that this concept might sound too apologetic (making excuses for or being too forgiving to those who've done us wrong), especially for readers who've been deeply harmed by others' transgressions. To that end, I want to acknowledge that there is a season to be hurt and angry. There is always space to grieve and own that what happened was not OK. However, my journey with Steps 8 and 9 helped me see that when I focused only on the ways I was harmed and hurt by others, that fueled my bad choices and behaviors. Hurt people tend to hurt people.

My hurt led me to behave in ways that didn't match my values and goals. A few of my maladaptive methods of responding were passive or direct aggression, emotional abuse, and acting out of spite. I wanted blood for my injustices. I would writhe with righteous indignation. I found temporary power and control in anger and victimization. Unfortunately, I'm fairly sure that even the safe, supportive people in my life found me difficult to be around during those seasons of my life. And the temporary power I felt quickly turned into more hurt and loneliness.

This abated as I worked Steps 8 and 9. The more I focused on making amends for when my responses and behaviors were outside my boundaries, the more at peace I felt with what had happened. I found that when someone wrongs me, lies to me, hurts me, I have a choice about how I want to respond. I learned that the bad behavior of others does not cancel out or excuse my own bad behavior. If my partner cheats on me with another married person and I—in my own pain and hurt—go out and start an affair with a married man "because no one honored my marriage vows so why should I respect others," then I am still 100 percent at fault for cheating, lying, and all the consequences that follow. Life is not a retaliatory game that somehow makes me not responsible for my choices and behaviors. I always have to live with the choices I've made, regardless of what has been done to me.

In our journey toward change, our egos are at first too fragile to make appropriate amends. Basically, we are not ready to own how we've harmed others. Our souls are drowning in hurt, rejection, and shame from everything going belly up. Our defenses are high, our nervous systems are a wreck, and we're unable to think or act in ways congruent to our values and goals. However, the more we try to humble ourselves, clean up our side of the street, and realize that we're all struggling in various ways, the more likely we are to acknowledge our own part in what our lives have become.

For non-addicts, the purpose of Steps 8 and 9 is less about repairing the damage we've done and more about softening our hearts and expanding our capacity for empathy and compassion. For me, the process of working Steps 8 and 9 allowed me to see that all of the transgressions that occurred within my marriage and beyond—either big and traumatic or part of everyday imperfections and unhealthy dynamics—were simply a part of what happens when two very flawed people try to engage in a long-term relationship. And that knowledge was a key element of my moving forward in healthier, more life-affirming ways.

Practicing Compassion, Self-Compassion, and Empathy

People are not born naturally empathetic and compassionate. These skills are learned and practiced. The following is an adapted outline to help you better understand the importance of practicing empathy and compassion, and to develop tools to implement these skills. (This material is adapted from *The Mindful Self-Compassion Workbook* by Dr. Kristin Neff and Dr. Christopher Germer, and *Rising Strong* by Dr. Brené Brown.)

- **Compassion** is not a hierarchical dynamic where one healed and whole person helps a wounded, less-whole person. Compassion is a shared recognition that we all hurt, we all suffer, we all need others for support at one time or another. Self-compassion is recognizing this in ourselves and practicing kindness.
- **Empathy** is the act of feeling *with* someone. It is understanding what someone is experiencing and then reflecting

it back to that person. We can use empathy to show compassion and to respond to others in a meaningful and caring way.

The following are guidelines to practice empathy and compassion with ourselves and others:

- **Stay Out of Judgment.** Judgment is often an extension of our own shame. When we're in struggle and shame about something, it is common to watch others and to judge their decisions, choices, and priorities with a hope that we can prove to ourselves that we're "better" or at least "not as bad as them." This is a huge obstacle to empathy.
- **Take Perspective.** We need to have a critical awareness of the lens that we're seeing things through. People's choices and behaviors are often a reflection of their own struggles, shame, and priorities. We must see their perspective as separate from ours. We are all working from different backgrounds and experiences. We must try to see their perspective.
- **Recognize the Emotions Involved.** What are we feeling as we hear the story? What is the other person feeling? Is it anger, sadness, joy, annoyance, frustration, gratitude? We must connect with the emotion they might be experiencing, not the situation they are describing.
- **Communicate the Feeling.** We should share what we think the other person is experiencing: "It sounds like you're (insert identified emotions here)." We do not have to be accurate. It simply shows that we're trying to track them and connect with their emotional experience.
- **Practice Mindfulness.** We need to be aware of what's going on in our body without letting that define us. We should pay attention to how practicing empathy and compassion is impacting us.
- **Practice Boundaries.** We can't be "in it to fix it." If we

don't practice boundaries while practicing empathy and compassion, our attempts can become exhausting, manipulative, or more shameful. Difficult events and feelings can't be wiped away or immediately fixed. A large part of the healing process is sitting with the pain.

- **Be Willing to Circle Back.** Empathy is a practice, so we will screw it up, fall short, miss an opportunity to show up for ourselves or another. If so, we can always go back and clean it up. There's no expiration date on empathy or compassion.

Things to Remember When Making Amends

Making amends is as much about practicing self-love and shame resiliency as it is about attempting to heal other's wounds. It hurts us to hurt others. A large part of recovery or getting to that "better place" emotionally and mentally stems from the ability to share our shame and own our imperfections, especially with those who have been harmed by them.

Therefore, when deciding what amends to make, we must explore our shame. We must plug into our hearts and minds to determine where we're still holding onto our hurt, pain, and shame voices. For example, I hold deep shame and hurt around how sarcastic and sharp-tongued I can be with my loved ones. When I fall short and speak to them in a less-than-desirable way, I partially make amends because I love them and I feel regretful for hurting them with my words or sentiment. I also make amends to validate that what I did was not OK. However, part of my amends comes from an internal desire to call myself out on what I've done so I don't get sucked into a vortex of deeper shame and torment where I continue to speak harshly and do more damage. Shameful acts beget more shame. If shame is not owned and shared, it will only grow and fester.

Addicts have sponsors and their 12-Step community to consult with when exploring who to make amends to and how to best make amends. If you have a 12-Step sponsor in a program for non-addicts like Prodependence Anonymous or Al-Anon, please consult with that individual before attempting any amends. If you're not in a 12-Step program, consult with a therapist who is familiar with the 12 Steps and understands how to work them. If you can't find anyone else, find an addict in recovery and ask if they will help you with Steps 8 and 9. Whatever you do, *do not undertake Steps 8 and 9 without supervision*. If you do so, your efforts may backfire, and you may create more damage than you clean up.

The following are a few things to consider when exploring Steps 8 and 9:

- There's a thin line between making amends for "pure" reasons (i.e., to practice shame resiliency, to practice self-love, and to repair the harm that's been done) and making amends because, deep down, you have manipulative intentions. Explore the "why" behind your amends.
- Are you making amends for your healing and your soul? Does the desire to make amends come from a place of vulnerability, humbleness, and authenticity? Or is it for pride and to save face?
- Your Higher Power is your source of forgiveness and love. Humans aren't always capable of forgiving others for their transgressions. If your amends is not well-received by the other person, your Higher Power will still appreciate it (as long as your motivations are pure).

Remember: You can't change the past and you can't control others. You can only own what is yours, accept the consequences for your choices, and when you know better, do better.

The purpose of Steps 8 and 9 is not to release your guilt or receive forgiveness from others. When you understand that, you can set clear boundaries before making amends to those you've harmed. When you make amends, speak the truth, only the facts, no excuses. No matter what, make amends without wounding another person further. And remember, the person you're making amends to is not responsible for forgiving you or making you feel better.

Steps 8 and 9, Exercise 1: Exploring What Gets in the Way of Empathy

Below we have listed some common errors that non-addicts make when practicing empathy and compassion with themselves and others. Please create a more empathic/compassionate response to the following:

Indicating That Feelings of Shame are Warranted

Example: Oh my gosh, you really did that? That's horrible. How embarrassed are you?

More Empathic Response: ______________________________

____

Responding with Sympathy Instead of Empathy

Example: You poor thing. I can't believe that happen to you. You must feel awful.

More Empathic Response: ______________________________

____

Expressing Disappointment and Judgment Rather Than Understanding

Example: How could you do such a thing? What were you thinking?

More Empathic Response:______________________________

____

Minimizing or Comparing the Situation

Example: Oh, you think that was bad? Please, that's not a big deal. You should hear the stuff that's happened to me.

More Empathic Response:________________________________

____

Steps 8 and 9, Exercise 2: Guided Imagery

As you prepare to make amends, go to a safe, quiet place, relax, put your hand on your heart, and explore the following:

- Imagine speaking to those with whom you seek to make amends.
- Imagine what you'd like to say to them.
- Imagine what their response might be.
- How would those responses make you feel?
- Are you OK if you don't get the response you're hoping for?
- What's the best possible outcome from such an exchange?
- What's the worst possible outcome?
- Are you prepared to cope with either scenario?

Write about your experience with this process, including ways you plan to cope with particular outcomes.

____

____

____

____

____

You Just Never Understand Me

Jennifer was an exhausted mother of two teenage girls. She sought therapy for her struggles with raising her girls in a single-family household while her ex-husband was remarried with a blended family. "These days my girls are angry about everything. It used to just be about the divorce, but now it's that I'm too strict about their curfews, that I don't allow them to have enough screen time, and that no other parents make their kids do as much as I make them do."

During what eventually amounted to weekly arguments, Jennifer would feel herself get furious as her girls complained, thinking about how hard she works to provide them clothing, vacations, and fun events, how she never signed up to be a single mother, and how good the girls have it compared to her childhood.

In therapy, Jennifer acknowledged she would lose her temper quickly. She increasingly felt dread on the days she'd pick her kids up from school. She was desperate for skills to de-escalate her chaotic home environment.

Through practice and hard work, Jennifer eventually adopted healthier communication skills, shame resiliency, and the ability to use empathy and compassion with her daughters during difficult conversations. She learned that even though she didn't agree with everything her daughters were saying to her, she could still "listen to understand" instead of "listening to respond." She would ask them more questions about their experiences, have them offer solutions to problems, and ask them to share their feelings in lieu of only defending herself and feeling attacked. She established ground rules with her daughters for communicating and interacting with one another: no name-calling, no screaming at one another, allowing each other to take breaks when discussions get too heated. Jennifer reminded them that it's OK to have different perspectives and points of view, and that occasionally they might have to agree to disagree.

Jennifer's practice of incorporating shame resiliency, empathy, and compassion into difficult conversations with her daughters allowed her to feel less attacked. It also provided an opportunity for her daughters to share their thoughts and feelings. There continued to be unsettled arguments and disagreements. However, even in adversity, they were able to share their differences of opinion safely and openly. "If nothing else," Jennifer says, "our new way of communicating is setting a better precedent for their future relationships."

Step 10 for Addicts

Continued to take personal inventory, and when we were wrong promptly admitted it.

Step 10, in most respects, is the logical culmination of the previous nine steps. In essence, the first nine steps are about stopping the bleeding of addiction and then identifying and cleaning up the wreckage of the addict's past. Step 10 begins the process of living differently in the present. Essentially, it is an ongoing version of Steps 4 through 9, wherein addicts take a quick inventory of a situation, identify their part in it, and, when necessary, either self-correct or quickly make an amends.

Happily, having worked Steps 4 through 9 already, addicts are familiar with this "inventory, assessment, change, and amends" process. The difference here is that Step 10 inventories deal with the present rather than the past, and the schedule for self-correcting or making an amends is "as soon as possible" rather than waiting until the addict is spiritually fit and the time is right.

Step 10 inventories deal with the present rather than the past, and the schedule for self-correcting or making an amends is "as soon as possible" rather than waiting until the addict is spiritually fit and the time is right.

For most addicts, Step 10 is a very unnatural process. Active addicts rarely (if ever) engage in self-examination and criticism. In fact, they avoid it like the plague. Even in recovery, many addicts sidestep or delay the process, putting off their Step 4 inventory for weeks or months, sometimes even years. Of course, having finally completed Steps 4 through 9, they now know the relief that self-examination and self-correction brings, and they are able to approach Step 10 with much less trepidation.

Unlike most of the previous steps, Step 10 is one that is worked on an ongoing basis, usually every day, sometimes more than once per day. In fact, Steps 10, 11, and 12 are all "daily practice" activities. For this reason, these steps are often referred to as "maintenance steps." The basic idea is that Steps 1 through 9 will get addicts sober and spiritually fit, and Steps 10 through 12 will keep them that way. Yes, lots of recovering addicts do go back and re-work earlier steps (especially Steps 4 and 5), but usually that is done on an annual basis or some other quite spread-out schedule. Steps 10, 11, and 12 are meant to be worked regularly.

Usually, Step 10 is done on an as-needed basis *and* at the end of each day. Let us examine the as-needed, spot-check inventory first. This type of tenth step recognizes that if you are disturbed or upset, then there is something wrong with either you or the situation around you and the issue is best looked at right away, before things escalate. For instance, if you are at work and become angry with your boss, a fellow employee, or a client, you can do a quick tenth step, pausing to look at the situation, making note of any part that you have played in it. Once you have a better understanding of what is happening and your role in it, you can more easily deal with it in an appropriate fashion.

Recovering addicts who learn to *pause before acting* in order to perform a quick tenth step inventory find that doing so typically prevents the sort of regrettable behaviors that later require a formal amends. For many, the short version of a Step 10 spot-check is "stop, breathe, think, breathe, and then proceed." Eventually, doing spot-check Step 10 inventories becomes a reflex reaction to all uncomfortable situations. When this occurs, life is much less troublesome and significantly more serene.

Most recovering addicts also work Step 10 at the end of each day, looking back upon the events that have passed and assessing how they did. Here the addict looks at situations that were handled with class and dignity, as well as situations in which he or she would hope to do better in the future. Occasionally, addicts realize they owe someone an amends. In such cases, they should make that amends as soon as possible—either right away if it's not too late in the evening or as soon as possible the following morning.

This end-of-day inventory is a way for addicts to keep their side of the street clean on an ongoing basis. It is also a way to uncover character defects they may not have been previously aware of.

Oftentimes, end-of-day Step 10 inventories are performed as part of the addict's daily spiritual practice. The concept of a daily spiritual practice will be discussed more thoroughly with Step 11. For now, I will simply reiterate that Step 10 is not a step taken once and forgotten; instead, it is an ongoing, day-to-day (sometimes even moment-to-moment) tool of recovery.

Step 10 for Non-Addicts

Continued to take personal inventory, and when we were wrong promptly admitted it.

By the time we've reached Step 10, we've done some deep, impactful work on our minds, souls, and relationships with others. In fact, the "Big Book" of Alcoholics Anonymous, after discussing Steps 1 through 9, lists the many benefits and changes one can expect from completing those steps, including, among other gains: experiencing newfound freedom, joy, and serenity; acceptance of the past; improved relationship dynamics and skills; reconnection with one's intuition and spirituality; the ability to let go of shame, suffering, and the need for comparison. Essentially, by working Steps 1 through 9 our attitudes and perspectives will shift and our paths will change. However, no benefit that is gained from this life-dissecting process of the 12-Step journey can sustain itself without Step 10.

Step 10 acknowledges that transformation is infinite and growth is on a continuum. Every day, we must remain aware of our propensity to slip back into our default, unhealthy habits. Therefore, we must continue to take personal inventory—weekly, daily, even hourly.

Being human is a permanent condition. There's no cure for our imperfections or struggles, at least not while we're on this earth. The closest we can get to true recovery is an ongoing commitment to do the best we can based on what we know at the time. To this end, we must be willing to continuously assess our behavior and choices, to learn from them, and to make amends when necessary. When we know better, we must do better. That's it.

As imperfect humans, we tend to make forward progress, then fall back. The essential piece is that we must consciously, humbly, and without defensiveness work toward forward progress as best we can, as often as we can. Everyone screws up to various degrees. The real damage (the lasting damage) is typically done only when we refuse to acknowledge our mistakes and make amends.

When I transcended my personal crises using the concepts of the 12 Steps as guideposts, I didn't come out the other end wearing a halo with roses and sunshine lining my path. My relationships (and relationship dynamics) remain extremely imperfect. I shove my foot in my mouth regularly. And I *constantly* wonder if I'm the biggest imposter in the world as I *attempt* to parent my children, work with clients as a therapist, and engage in intimate relationships with my family and friends.

As I do these things, I try to remember that *shame* and the *fear* of being unloved and unwanted are as omnipresent and irreversible in me as my innate drive to seek connection with others. I simply can't experience one without the other. As long as I have a desire to love and be loved by others, I'm going to have a little voice inside my head saying, "Um, I don't know Kristin, are you sure you deliver a package that is actually something others like and want to have around?"

Shame and the _fear_ of being unloved and unwanted are as omnipresent and irreversible in me as my innate drive to seek connection with others. I simply can't experience one without the other.

Therefore, when I'm being mindful of my behaviors and choices, I ask myself, "If my shame and fear have me on trial all day, every day, trying to convince me that I'm a crappy human who's not valuable, am I behaving in ways that give my shame and fear more evidence to support that theory? Or am I acting in ways that provide evidence to the contrary?" This concept might sound a bit transactional—be good to feel good—but it helps me hit the pause button and develop a clearer path toward congruent decision-making, which is what Step 10 is all about.

Speaking of Step 10, I find the following process useful when working it. When exploring my decisions and behaviors (taking personal inventory), I ask myself two basic questions:

1. Is this particular behavior congruent with my values and goals?
2. Do I have to lie or manipulate in order to execute or maintain this particular behavior?

The answers to those questions typically lead me toward the most congruent path.

There are a set of guideposts I use to help me through my daily inventory. These guideposts are a loose adaptation of Dr. Brené Brown's BRAVING model presented in her book, *Rising Strong*. I use these guideposts to evaluate my interactions with others—my words, my actions, and my choices. This helps me determine my part in a problem and where I might need to make amends or revisit something.

- **Authenticity:** Did I show up for myself and others? Am

I consistent in this regard? Was I manipulative, defensive, or "fake" in any way?

- **Boundaries:** Was I clear with others about what's OK and what's not OK? Am I aware of what I need and what I experienced, and did I communicate that clearly to those involved? At the same time, was I able to hear and respect others' boundaries?
- **Accountability:** Did I explore where I might have fallen short? Did I respond to others appropriately or from a reactive place? What do I need to do to clean up my side of the street?
- **Integrity:** Did I *practice* my values rather than *profess* them? Did I behave in a way that fully honors and is integrated with my values, goals, and priorities?
- **Nonjudgment:** Do I create an environment where I can be present for other's experiences and stories without judging them? Do I have people around me where I can share my story openly and freely without feeling shamed or judged?
- **Benefit of the Doubt:** Do I try my best to maintain the idea that most people are doing the best they can with what they've been given?
- **Self-Care and Gratitude:** Am I taking steps to maintain my mental health and well-being by practicing gratitude (thankfulness and appreciation) as often as possible, with all things?

Taken together, my two questions and the aforementioned guidelines can help us stay mindful, aware, and in the executive functioning part of our brain. That is the state where we make good choices, feel connected to others, and consider the consequences of our actions in broader contexts.

Our default, unconscious state allows shame and fear to drive our choices, causing us to behave in narrow-minded, unhelpful ways.

As Richard Rohr states in *Breathing Under Water*, "Whenever we do anything stupid, cruel, evil, or destructive to ourselves or others, we are at the moment unconscious, and unconscious of our identity. If we are fully conscious, we would never do it." So we must work hard to remain conscious and to move away from the default, reactive state that leads us astray.

Step 10 reminds us to never underestimate the persistency of our old, wretched habits. It's a constant process of embracing our eternally flawed condition while never ceasing in our efforts to change it and improve upon it. In other words: Step 10 is the personification of the much-used recovery phrase: Progress, not perfection.

Step 10, Exercise 1: Taking Inventory

Think of current, stressful situations you are dealing with (involving dynamics within yourself and with others). These situations can be marital issues, problems at work, issues with family, personal struggles, etc. Then answer the following questions.

What is (was) your initial reaction when faced with this stressor or this person? Defensive? Shut down? Ignore it? Minimize it? Blame it on someone else? Get angry?

____

____

____

As you explore your initial reaction, where do you feel it in your body? What would you call that feeling in your body? There can be multiple feelings—mad, sad, afraid, hurt, anxious, paralyzed, weak, damaged, broken, etc.

____

____

____

How do you feel like you should have reacted to this stressor? How would a reasonable person respond to this situation?

____

____

____

What are the potential obstacles to your ideal response in these situations? Is there previous trauma coming up for you? Resentments or grudges involving this person or issue? Do you feel guilty or ashamed about something related to the issue?

____

____

____

Process your thoughts and experience with your support system and Higher Power. Explore with them the guideposts provided earlier. After this exploration, what do you feel is an appropriate reaction to this issue? Are others seeing something that you might be missing? Can they help you with any blind spots? What are your values and goals related to this issue?

____

____

____

Do you need to clean up your side of the street in any way? Have you done something outside your boundaries, commitments, and values? What do you need to do to get back into integrity?

____

____

____

List preferred ways to do continued inventory/self-search—quiet time, daily walks, gratitude, meditation/prayer, support groups, yoga, etc. Why are each of these ways effective for you?

____

____

____

The Old Timer

Clarence Snyder was one of the original members of AA. His sponsor was Dr. Bob, the co-founder of AA. In a 1982 interview, Clarence discussed the genesis of the 12 Steps and AA in general—the meetings and the evolution of the program. In this conversation, he discussed the shift in the program from the 9th Step to the 10th Step. "After nine steps, we're new people," he says. "Step 10 is personal, not moral... daily activity... how we live today. I have to do this simple program. At night, I think about my day. What I did. Who I met. Did I do something worthwhile? Do I need to ask for forgiveness somewhere? First thing I take care of tomorrow. Do it promptly. Don't put it off."

Step 11 for Addicts

Sought through prayer and meditation to improve our conscious contact with God as we understood God, praying only for knowledge of God's will for us and the power to carry that out.

Step 11, like Step 10, is not a step that is worked once and then forgotten. Instead, it is part of an ongoing (usually daily) ritual of recovery. That said, recovering addicts often find "prayer" and "meditation" to be somewhat baffling concepts. And some, especially those who began the recovery process as agnostics or atheists, may still be struggling with the concept of having a Higher Power at all. For these reasons (and many others), Step 11 can be a difficult one to work. If addicts find themselves struggling with this step, they can take heart in the fact that they are very far from alone, for even the most devoutly religious members of 12-Step recovery groups sometimes temporarily lose their way here.

The good news is that if addicts have diligently worked the first ten steps and find themselves still at odds with the spiritual nature of recovery, that's OK. As mentioned above, Step 11 is part of an ongoing practice. As such, nobody is expected to work it perfectly. In fact, the *effort* of working Step 11 is usually far more important in terms of lasting positive effects than any other factor. The step itself actually takes this into account by incorporating the words "as we understood God." In other words, however it is that you understand (or don't understand) your Higher Power, that's just peachy. You don't have to be a devout Christian, Jew, Muslim, or anything else to work Step 11, because Step 11 isn't about religion.

Instead, it's about finding your personal spiritual center, whatever that might be.

For some addicts this is relatively easy, especially those who arrived in recovery with an existing spiritual practice. In such cases, a renewed effort in that discipline is usually the way to go. The exception to this occurs when an addict no longer trusts or believes in that discipline. This sometimes happens when the "religion of one's childhood" has a scary, judgmental, punishing form of God, or when the people associated with that religion did not adequately practice what they preached. In such cases, it is perfectly acceptable (from a 12-Step standpoint, anyway) to develop a completely different spiritual connection.

That said, for addicts who don't yet have a spiritual connection and for addicts who are seeking a different one, the mere thought of trying to find one can feel daunting. But it needn't, as the process is really not difficult. The only things required for success are open-mindedness and willingness, and by the time most recovering addicts reach Step 11, they are more than a little bit familiar with these tenets.

The first thing to understand is that there is no right or wrong way to develop a spiritual connection. There are as many ways to accomplish this task as there are people who've done it. In other words, no two people's journey and experience are exactly the same. And the real reward isn't reaching some specific spiritual plateau; it is simply making the journey and having the spiritual experience. Nevertheless, a few general tips may help addicts find *their pathway* toward enlightenment.

The first thing to understand is that there is no right or wrong way to develop a spiritual connection. There are as many ways to accomplish this task as there are people who've done it.

- **Make your spiritual quest a regular part of your daily routine.** Set aside a specific time each day where you will not be disturbed by family, work, or other outside distractions.
- **Create a "sacred space" in which to conduct your daily spiritual practice.** This may be something formal and elaborate such as a meditation garden, or it may be something quite simple, such as your favorite easy chair (with the television, music, phone, and other potential distractions either removed or turned off).
- **Develop a spiritual routine.** This could include a guided meditation, a series of affirmations, a specific or nonspecific prayer, writing out a gratitude list, etc.
- **If all else fails, find a spiritual mentor.** Pick someone who has what you want in terms of his or her spiritual connection and do what he or she does. Eventually, you will be able to adapt elements of that person's spiritual practice into your own.

Addicts should never be afraid to experiment with new ideas and to alter their spiritual practice as time passes. It is very likely that as they continue to work Step 11, their concept of a Higher Power will change, as will their ability to connect with it. Thus, their daily routine is likely to vary over time as a reflection of this growth.

Step 11 for Non-Addicts

Sought through prayer and meditation to improve our conscious contact with God as we understood God, praying only for knowledge of God's will for us and the power to carry that out.

Like many, I deeply struggled with concepts around prayer and meditation. As a Type A control freak, I found those behaviors to be unproductive and, therefore, a waste of time. I wanted to move quickly, burn lots of calories, look fabulous, perform, achieve, and win trophies. That's how I coped with the discomfort of life. Never being still, outperforming my shame voices, and chasing validation from others. That may not sound like a bad life to fellow over-achievers, but it didn't work for me because I had very little tolerance for anything remotely uncomfortable like hurt, criticism, uncertainty, or—God forbid—shame.

Sigmund Freud suggested that humans will go to great lengths to avoid feeling uncomfortable. When faced with stressors or uncertainties, our human condition will first and foremost seek out "relief" from the situation, rather than becoming fully aware of what's happening. Unfortunately, seeking relief tends to prevent us from properly assessing the circumstances, putting them through a filter of values and goals, and determining the healthiest way forward. Instead, the relief we seek often comes in the form of character defects that we listed in Step 5: over-spending, over-performing, under-functioning, controlling, manipulating, emotional instability, isolating, etc. Freud called these behaviors "defense mechanisms."

We all choose different forms of relief or escape. One person may jump from one toxic, intensity-filled relationship to the next. Another will seek power in angry outbursts and posturing threats toward others. Another will recoil, isolate, and disengage. These are very different behaviors on the surface, but they are all serving a similar purpose: to disconnect from pain, to distract, to create the appearance of having control where there is none, to numb out or check out. Unfortunately, we can be dangerous to ourselves and others when we're disconnected from ourselves and our Higher Power. This is why Step 11 is so important.

The Importance of Staying Conscious and Connected

With Step 10, I emphasized that a conscious, connected person who's fully cognizant of his/her actions and the consequences of those actions doesn't tend to make horrible life choices. People like that don't tend to rage at their loved ones or have an affair or relapse on drugs. It's when we're disconnected, consumed by uncomfortable feelings, and in shame or fear that we behave in ways that are incongruent with our goals and values.

It's when we're disconnected, consumed by uncomfortable feelings, and in shame or fear that we behave in ways that are incongruent with our goals and values.

Being conscious, connected, and mindful is being fully integrated and aware of your thoughts, your feelings, the sensations in your body, your environment, the people around you, your goals, values, and intentions, and remaining curious about all of those moving parts. That is what I mean when I say "connected."

It's imperative that we stay as conscious and connected as possible. That is the purpose of Step 11: To provide a path and practice for us to remain aligned and engaged with our self and our Higher Power (whatever that is to us). The longer we remain in unconscious states of hurt, pain, or struggle, the more difficult Step 11 becomes. Without daily intervention, we might become stuck in a vicious cycle of disconnection and suffering. And only our ability to use healthy, congruent coping skills (such as Step 11) can help us transcend those states.

Step 11 suggests a *regular practice* of praying or connecting with ourselves and our Higher Power. That daily practice can help us feel more empowered and prepared for when the shit hits the fan. Similar to the way the military drills their soldiers over and over to make sure they're prepared to perform during intense situations, people in recovery must remain committed to practicing Step 11 to stay congruent and integrated. That is how we make it through intense situations. Through a connection with our Higher Power, we can find peace and clarity in our path forward, along with a reminder of our values, goals, and motivations.

As stated earlier, I initially struggled with the idea of prayer and meditation. It's taken years of convincing and continued research to open my heart and mind to engaging with my Higher Power. Initially, I lacked a true *belief* in prayer, meditation, or a Higher Power, but I nevertheless found the *practice* of prayer and meditation to be helpful in slowing me down, helping me remember what I was working toward and the characteristics I wanted to embody. Eventually, continued exploration of Step 11 led me to a greater appreciation for the roles that prayer, meditation, and connection can play in mental health, relationships, and stability.

For many people, actions like prayer, meditation, and mindfulness feel familiar and comforting. For others, however, including both Scott and me, when we first embarked on our recovery journeys, words like "prayer" and "God" could cause a shutdown. So contemplating Step 11 can initially trigger everything from relief and peace to disdain and cynicism, depending on one's history and experience with religion and spirituality.

While Scott and I understand the objections people often have to Step 11, we have both learned through observation, personal practice, and professional research that prayer, meditation, and connection are basic human needs that transcend religious establishments and theological constructs. As a result, we believe that monotheists, polytheists, spiritualists, agnostics, and even atheists can benefit from Step 11. So, despite any preconceived notions you may have about religion, God, Higher Power, or spirituality, I'm asking you to remain open to Step 11's suggestions.

What the Experts Say

Dr. Stephen Porges, Dr. Brené Brown, and Dr. Bessel Van der Kolk all provide evidence-based practices for calming our threat/shame states and returning to executive functioning and stability. Their lists include (and please pay special attention to the first two items on the list):

MENU OF EMOTIONAL REGULATION OPTIONS/HEALTHY COPING SKILLS

Grounding techniques	Eating right
Mindfulness meditation	Avoiding substance use/abuse
Visualizations	Tapping arms or legs rhythmically
Body Scan/Progressive Relaxation	Journaling
Breathwork	Gratitude
Dance/movement	Talking to a trusted person
Tai chi/qui gong	Going out in nature
Yoga	Performing community service
Pets/animal therapy	Neurofeedback
Sleep	Social engagement
Exercise	Healthy/safe touch (hugs, massage, etc.)
Singing	Big sighs
Playing an Instrument	Screaming into a pillow
Exercising	Hitting a punching bag
Talk therapy	Participating in a support group

As you can see from the above list, there are numerous ways to move into a more connected state. One of the best, and one that is facilitated by 12-Step recovery, is to seek the comfort of others who understand us and can help us regulate our emotions and behaviors in times of stress and struggle. Conscious. Connected. Comforted. This is how Step 11 is part of an evidence-based practice, not just some sort of crazy spiritual superstition or a cultish religion.

Why Step 11 Works

We are emotional creatures who are often driven by unconscious/subconscious thoughts and feelings. The individuals who developed the 12 Steps knew we had to incorporate a regular practice of moving out of our unconscious, shame-filled, superficial choices and reactions and into more purposeful choices.

Incongruent people hurt people. Unconscious people hurt people. Prayer, meditation, mindfulness, breathwork, and other mind-body consciousness techniques can counteract this.

When we pray, we check in with ourselves and our Higher Power, we seek guidance, we check in with our heart and our intentions. This practice helps us remain (or become) congruent, conscious, and rational.

There are countless ways to practice Step 11, and you may need to experiment to find what works best for you. One of my most frequent prayers is that my heart will soften so I can be flexible, moving with the ebbs and flows of life. Before I worked Step 11, I would pray (if and when I prayed) for my Higher Power to be flexible, to bend to my hopes and wishes. So this new prayer is a big change for me, a change that helps me stay grounded, which is better not only for me but for those with whom I'm in relationship.

I still struggle with uncertainty and vulnerability, of course. Everyone does. I just know now that it's useless to try to engineer those human experiences out of my life. I also understand that without mystery and vulnerability, I would miss out on what makes life real, engaging, complex, beautiful, and, yes, difficult.

Still Struggling?

Clients often tell me they want recovery, but they just don't think the 12 Steps are for them. "Fine," I say. "Just find another group of people that you can regularly meet with who think similarly enough to you so that they can call you on your shit. And make sure you all create a space where you can speak freely, without fear of judgment or exploitation."

To me, that is the essence of Step 11—a safe, intimate, empathetic, and honest environment that keeps us on track, connected to and congruent with our values and goals. As long as we feel a loving connection and presence that helps us release our shame and stay as congruent and connected as possible, we are effectively working Step 11. That space may involve a traditional god and religion, or not. How we go about working this step is not important; what's important is that we do it.

Step 11, Exercise 1: Neurobiology 101 and Polyvagal Theory

Understanding our neurobiology is synonymous with understanding addiction and the unhealthy coping skills we seek. We are constantly affected by our autonomic nervous system—an unconscious, involuntary, quick-processing system housed in our brain and spine that is constantly scanning our environment to determine what is threatening or unsafe. This highly efficient system scans people, faces, places, sounds, odors, etc., sending messages to our body about what's OK and what's not OK.

That said, every human has different cues of safety or threat. These individualized cues are shaped by our life experiences. Any person, thing, or event could be interpreted as a potential threat by our nervous system, depending on what we've previously encountered.

Dr. Stephen Porges calls these cues our "neuroception." Dr. Porges says that neuroception is the messages we receive from our *unconscious* neurobiology. He contrasts neuroception with perception, which is information driven by our *conscious* thoughts and feelings. Despite the fact that neuroception and perception are very separate messaging systems, we rarely realize that in the moment. Confusing the two message systems can have disastrous consequences.

There are three main states for our autonomic nervous system:

- **The Ventral Vagal State**: When a person's body feels stable, connected to their thoughts/feelings, and fully present with other people, experiences, animals, etc.
- **The Sympathetic State**: When a person's body enters a "fight or flight" state with an overwhelming need to "mobilize" or "do something" about a potential threat.
- **The Dorsal State**: When a person's body enters an overwhelmed, shut-down, "freeze" state of hopelessness. When the person becomes immobilized by fear or discomfort.

Each of these states sends unconscious, involuntary cues to the brain, and the brain tries to make sense of the possible threat by "writing a story" about what's happening. The "story" isn't always accurate. It's often based on an overgeneralized scenario from the past or our shame voices. The story (or perception) the brain creates can trigger our defense mechanisms, firing up our shame voices further, wreaking havoc on relationship dynamics.

This type of unhelpful response occurs because the prefrontal, executive functioning parts of our brain shut down or are limited during Sympathetic and Dorsal states. That means our brains will struggle to write an accurate story that will help us defend ourselves in a healthy way. Instead, we lash out, or flee, or freeze.

The Sympathetic and Dorsal states are helpful to our survival if we're facing a real and serious threat of bodily harm. But most often, our threat-response system is triggered by past trauma and misinterpretation, which can push us toward emotional instability, poor coping skills, and behaviors that are incongruent with our values and goals.

Sympathetic and Dorsal threat states need very little oxygen and very little blood supply to hijack the executive functioning parts of our brain. It takes a ton of effort, however, for our brain to engage the Ventral Vagal state where rational thought, good judgment, and impulse control are front and center. A Ventral Vagal state is necessary for our brain to properly vet decisions, weigh the potential consequences of our actions, and make good choices.

Interestingly, one of the most effective ways to achieve a Ventral Vagal state is to practice Step 11. And for many people, actions like prayer, meditation, gratitude, and mindfulness feel familiar and comforting.

Think of incidences where you were in each of the states: Ventral Vagal, Sympathetic, and Dorsal Vagal. How would you describe each of those states? If you named that state, what would it be? Examples: annoyed, petrified, in love, connected, peaceful, harmonious, blank.

Ventral: ____

____

Sympathetic: ____

____

Dorsal: ____

____

Describe how your body feels in each of those states. Examples: fiery, twitching, numb.

Ventral: ____

____

Sympathetic: ____

____

Dorsal: ____

____

What is the story you tend to tell yourself in each of these states? Example: I'm failing/scared/falling apart/embarrassed/going to run away from everyone.

Ventral: ____

____

Sympathetic: ____

____

Dorsal: ____

___

What are some potential coping skills you could use in each of these states?

Ventral: ___

___

Sympathetic: ___

___

Dorsal: ___

___

Step 11, Exercise 2: A Restorative Meditation Practice

Meditation is the art of training your brain to enter a state of calm concentration and positive emotions. Research shows that practicing meditation for even ten minutes a day can help with the following:

- Less rumination.
- Reduced stress.
- Improved memory.
- Better focus.
- Greater emotional regulation/control.
- Improved self-reflection.
- Higher relationship satisfaction.

The following are a few different forms of meditation that you can try:

- **Meditative/Therapeutic Breathing:** This is the most accessible and foundational form of meditation. "Box breathing" is the act of inhaling for three seconds, holding it for three seconds, exhaling for three seconds, holding it for three seconds, and then repeating the cycle. Regularly practicing this form of breathing can train the brain and body to down-regulate during stress and improve focus.
- **Mindfulness Meditation:** This is the practice of being present and aware without judging the moment or getting distracted by thoughts or concerns. Sit down or lay down, relax, pay attention to your breath and your body. As your mind wanders, refocus on your breath and the sensations in your body. Start slowly: one minute, then two, then five. Your ability to be mindful will improve with time.
- **Guided Imagery:** This is a great way to meditate if you struggle with stillness. It can be done with audio

> instruction that leads you through the process. The guided imagery can take you to peaceful places, help you imagine reaching and achieving goals, or it can have an empowerment theme to it. Whatever works for you.

If you are new to these processes, expect your initial attempts to be still, meditate, and connect with yourself and your Higher Power to be difficult. A minute of stillness may feel excruciating, like attempting to run a mile after years of being out-of-shape and sedentary. But the ability to be still and mindful is a muscle that can build in strength. This is why meditation is considered a practice. There are thousands of helpful resources (apps, articles, books) that can help you to learn more about meditation and to begin a structured, regular practice.

Try one or more of these forms of meditation every day for a week and write about your experience in the space below.

____

____

____

____

____

Steve was an officer in the Navy and deployed often as a part of his service. As Steve prepared to retire from the military, he discovered texts and emails exposing years of infidelity by his wife of eighteen years, Susan. She'd had several affairs with different men, most often while he was deployed and serving his country.

The discovery was devastating to Steve, but he insisted that "failure was not an option" and that he and his wife wanted to repair, recover, and move forward from the betrayal. Susan engaged in the repair process with humility and accountability. She provided a full disclosure of her history of acting out with other men, began a 12-Step recovery program for love addiction, and did in-depth therapy to better understand her acting out patterns and history.

Despite all of Susan's willingness and work, the betrayal trauma wrought by years of lying, gaslighting, and cheating ate away ay Steve's self-esteem, his willingness to be vulnerable again, and his hope for repair. "I just can't do it," he would say during difficult couple's therapy sessions. "I love her but I hate her. I just don't know how I will ever be able to trust her or feel safe with her again."

Steve's struggle is a common one, especially after suffering such long-term, evasive betrayal. For years, Steven (understandably and naturally) will continue to grapple with trusting his wife. After all, he's seen her at her worst, he knows what she's capable of, so he'll remain unsure of when she might relapse and return to her "old behaviors." This is why Step 11 can be such an important practice in the healing process.

No one can *guarantee* that bad stuff will stop happening. Addicts relapse. Betrayed partners may be betrayed again. People lie, hurt others, and behave selfishly. These are vulnerabilities we're exposed to every day with all of our relationships. Step 11 reminds us that we have to purposely and explicitly engage our Higher Power to receive the help, support, and love of a power greater than our flawed human condition. A daily practice of "surrendering" to these uncertainties with prayer, meditation, and engagement with our Higher Power reminds us that life is out of our control and we will naturally struggle with managing it. Therefore, we need to trust a "new" manager.

While Steve and Susan worked to rebuild some semblance of

trust, Steve leaned heavily on his Higher Power for support because that was the only thing he was willing to trust for a while. Happily, through a program of rigorous honesty, Susan eventually re-earned his trust. But even then, Steve held firmly to his faith in a Higher Power, knowing that entity could and would see him through even the worst of times.

Step 12 for Addicts

Having had a spiritual awakening as the result of these steps, we tried to carry this message to other alcoholics [or addicts], and to practice these principles in all our affairs.

The first thing addicts should do when they approach Step 12 is to recognize the first portion of the step's language, "Having had a spiritual awaking as the result of these steps." In other words, by the time they reach Step 12, they will have had a spiritual awakening of some sort. Most likely it was not of the burning bush variety, but no doubt they've experienced it. Addicts who think they haven't simply need to take a quick inventory, asking themselves:

- Have I stopped my addictive behavior?
- Am I interacting in healthier ways with family members, bosses, co-workers, neighbors, and random strangers?
- Do I feel better about myself and my place in the world?
- Am I more accepting of others?

If the answer to these questions is "yes" (or even "sometimes"), and it almost certainly is if they've diligently worked the first 11 steps, then they have indeed had a spiritual awakening. If so, addicts can pause for a moment and pat themselves on the back, because they are ready for the remainder of Step 12.

The remainder of Step 12 can be broken down into two parts:

1. Helping others to recover from addiction.

2. Practicing the 12-Step principles in all their affairs.

First let us discuss helping others. This can be done in numerous ways. Often, people think sponsorship of newcomers is the only route, but it is not. Certainly, however, it is one of the best. And it is relatively simple. A sponsor's job is to understand the newcomer's addiction issues as thoroughly as possible, and to guide that individual through the process of working the 12 Steps. (If the addict is a first-time sponsor and unsure of the route, he or she can consult with his or her own sponsor about how to handle things.)

Another great way to work Step 12 is to attend and participate in 12-Step meetings. By simply attending 12-Step meetings, addicts are supporting others on the recovery journey, letting them know they are not alone and that their fellows care about them. When addicts talk in a meeting, which is highly encouraged, they share their experience, strength, and hope, allowing others to learn and benefit from both their errors and their successes.

By simply attending 12-Step meetings, addicts are supporting others on the recovery journey, letting them know they are not alone and that their fellows care about them.

Even people who are uncomfortable talking in meetings can be of service by arriving early to help set up chairs and make coffee, and staying late to clean up. These "quiet workers" are the people who make AA meetings possible. The trick with service work, as twelfth step work is often called, is finding a "job" that one is comfortable with, and then doing it without expecting recognition or thanks.

The second part of Step 12, practicing the 12-Step principles in all their affairs, is even easier. After all, they've been doing this with their addiction and most of their day-to-day life already, and they have Step 10 (which they practice on a regular basis) to keep them on the straight and narrow. In Step 12, they merely continue implementing the step-work they've already done and are doing on an ongoing basis, applying the lessons they've learned to all aspects of their existence, not just their addiction.

Despite the ease of working Step 12, recovering addicts nearly always fall short of their ultimate goals. And this is just fine. In fact, it's not only acceptable, it's expected. Addicts are not saints when they arrive in recovery, and they do not miraculously become saints just because they're working a program of recovery. The real goal is to live sober lives one day at a time, and to do that a little bit better today than yesterday.

Step 12 for Non-Addicts

Having had a spiritual awakening as the result of these steps, we tried to carry this message to others, and to practice these principles in all our affairs.

The Step 12 chapter of the Alcoholics Anonymous book *Twelve Steps and Twelve Traditions* is nearly twice as long as any of the chapters for the previous 11 steps. It's filled with a wealth of reminders, suggestions, cautionary tales, and guidelines on how to continue the work after "completing" the 12 Steps. It reminds us that the life-changing work of the steps will allow us to feel and experience things we were unable to experience before, and that we will find clarity and purpose in a life that was previously something to endure or "get through." The chapter also encourages us to apply the tools we learned with the first 11 steps to all current and future relationships and challenges. At the same time, it cautions us to avoid complacency and to maintain a path of personal growth to weather future storms of crisis, hurt, and devastation.

Most importantly, Step 12 highlights a core tenet of lasting recovery and stability: being of service to others. Countless historical figures, research studies, and books emphasize this same idea—that enduring happiness is found in giving to and helping others.

It is better to give than to receive.
—Acts 20:35

No one has ever become poor by giving.
—Anne Frank

Only by giving are you able to receive more than you already have.
—James Rohn

The Gift of Giving

Psychologists find that being of service is at the core of connection, vulnerability, and fulfillment. It allows us to make meaning from our traumas and grief. We also receive pleasure from service. In fact, brain imagery shows that altruism stimulates the same pleasure areas of the brain as food and sex.

Psychologists find that being of service is at the core of connection, vulnerability, and fulfillment. It allows us to make meaning from our traumas and grief.

The creators of the 12-Step model considered serving others such a significant piece of long-term sobriety that service was built into the framework of the program through the sponsor/sponsee structure. Accordingly, 12-Step group participants who've completed the steps and have established lasting sobriety are encouraged to assist newcomers by sponsoring them, helping them stay sober with useful advice and guidance through the 12 Steps.

Sponsorship is a mentoring system that not only helps newcomers, it reminds old-timers of what a return to active addiction might look like. It also causes sponsors to revisit the steps themselves, continuing their work of recovery and healing as they help others do the same. In this way, sponsorship serves a dual purpose: Sponsorship provides hope, accountability, and guidance to newcomers, while also helping those who've had a spiritual awakening as a result of completing the steps to remain engaged and invested in the ongoing process of recovery and healing.

Twelve-Step programs all acknowledge that growth is continuous while complacency can be dangerous. Addicts helping other addicts gives them meaning, purpose, and perspective while reminding them of the harrowing stories, challenges, and defense mechanisms that they can return to if they stop working their program and allow complacency to set in.

Non-addicts can benefit just as much as recovering addicts from serving others and remaining vigilant about complacency. However, the benefits of such good deeds will only be realized if they are offered within boundaries. Boundaries are guidelines or limits that a person sets when engaging with others, while also establishing appropriate responses when others pass or ignore those limits. Simply put: Boundaries are your definition of what is OK and what is not OK in your life and relationships.

The following is a helpful chart I use for teaching boundaries to clients. It helps you differentiate and identify healthy ways to engage with others while pointing out less-healthy ways of behaving with others.

Healthy Boundaries vs. Unhealthy Boundaries

Healthy Boundaries	**Unhealthy Boundaries**
You can say no or yes and you are OK when others say no to you.	You can't say no because you are afraid of rejection or abandonment.
You have a strong sense of identity. You respect yourself.	Your identity consists of what you think others want you to be. You are a chameleon.

Healthy Boundaries	Unhealthy Boundaries
You expect reciprocity in a relationship—you share responsibility and power.	You have no balance of power or responsibility in your relationships. You tend to be either overly responsible and controlling or passive and dependent.
You know when the problem is yours and when it belongs to someone else.	You take on other's problems as your own.
You share personal information gradually in a mutually sharing/trusting relationship.	You share personal information too soon—before establishing mutual trust/sharing.
You do not tolerate any form of abuse or disrespect.	You have a high tolerance for abuse and being treated with disrespect.
You know your own wants, needs, and feelings. You communicate them clearly.	Your wants, needs, and feelings are secondary to others and are sometimes determined by others.
You are committed to and responsible for exploring and nurturing your full potential.	You ignore your inner voice or instincts and allow others' expectations to define your potential.
You are responsible for your own happiness and fulfillment. You allow others to be responsible for their own happiness and fulfillment.	You feel responsible for others' happiness and fulfillment and sometimes rely on your relationships to create that for you.
You value your opinions, instincts, and feelings as much as (or more than) other people's opinions and feelings.	You tend to absorb the feelings of others. You rely on others' opinions, feelings, and ideas more than your own.
You know your limits (physically and emotionally). You allow others to define their own limits.	You allow others to define your limits in order to please them, or you try to define limits for others.
You are able to ask for help when you need it.	You feel that asking for help is a sign of weakness and you avoid it.
You don't compromise your values or integrity to avoid rejection or adversity.	You compromise your values and beliefs in order to please others or avoid conflict.

Some people believe that boundaries create obstacles to loving and giving to others. However, the empathy and compassion necessary for such acts flow more freely from those with strong boundaries. One must give to others without the weight of duty, obligation, or quid pro quo. Opting out of healthy boundaries can drain emotional resources, lead one to feel like a martyr, and contribute to resentment or passive aggression toward others. Such conditions would make it difficult to stay free of one's character defects and bad habits. And then you're back to Step 1. So remember, even when being of service, you must engage others within healthy boundaries.

The twelfth step winds down an intense journey of personal and relational work. It provides the framework and guidance to help you continue the path of growth while maintaining honesty, accountability, and stability. Completing the 12 Steps will never result in the end of adversity and challenges. Life will continue to present challenges and people will continue to disappoint. However, the 12 Steps provide you with the tools you need to transcend those moments with support, integrity, and purpose.

Step 12, Exercise 1: Creating Healthy Attachment with Yourself and Others

Early 19th century parenting experts believed that raising autonomous, confident, resourceful children required parents to keep "proper distance" from their child. Parents were to avoid "coddling them" by giving them too much attention, holding them, rocking them, or comforting them when they cried. However, after groundbreaking research by attachment theorists Mary Ainsworth and John Bowlby, it was found that children need love, affection, and secure attachments with safe adults as desperately as they require food and water for survival. The absence of secure attachment with others creates a lifetime of stunted physical, emotional, intellectual, and social development. (It can also be a core underlying issue in addiction.)

Fortunately, science has also shown that our brains are malleable (referred to as "neuroplasticity") and can repair trauma and attachment wounds. Developing secure attachment behaviors is paramount to engaging in and maintaining long-term healthy relationships. It's directly correlated with a willingness to take healthy risks, engage in creativity, and find satisfaction in life.

Developing Secure Attachment

The following are guideposts to practicing and engaging in secure attachment with others:

- **Come from a Place of Worthiness:** Assume that you are loveable, valuable, and that the people you are in relationship with see you as a positive part of their life. Also, give others the benefit of the doubt when it feels safe to do so.
- **Practice Effective Communication:** Clearly communicate your feelings and needs, allow others to do the same, avoid name-calling or generalizations. Do not avoid having difficult conversations just to "keep the peace." Listen

to understand, not to respond.

- **Be Predictable, Not Perfect:** Predictability equals safety; safety is required for intimacy; intimacy leads to secure attachment. Predictability comes from being honest, following through with your commitments and promises, and being consistent.
- **Seek Proximity to Others in Times of Pain and Joy:** Invest in and develop your close relationships at all seasons of your life. We need others during times of celebration and times of pain and suffering. Cues of safe connection can come from eye contact, voice tone, safe body language, and safe, consensual, predictable physical contact from others.
- **Giving and Receiving Comfort:** When being comforted by others or when you're comforting others, remember the guideposts of empathy and compassion. Comfort without judgment.
- **Don't Try to Fix It:** Pain avoidance isn't the goal. The goal is building a tolerance for pain and providing healthy coping tools to get through it.
- **See and Be Seen:** Attune to loved ones. Try to understand what they're feeling or experiencing so they can feel "seen." This can also be done by literally being seen, showing up for your loved one's events, engaging in hobbies together, spending quality time with one another. Being seen by others also requires you to share what's going on with you, helping loved ones understand your experience and reality.
- **Repair Mistakes in a Timely Manner:** Repair mistakes and damage as soon as possible. There will be imperfections and ruptures in all relationships. It's important that everyone invest in repairing and reconnecting.
- **Talk About Messy Things:** Humanity and vulnerability are inherently messy. Don't be afraid to have the difficult

conversations, to discuss scary, uncertain things. Doing so can help build resiliency within a relationship.

- **Always Stay Curious:** Narrate what you see, get curious about why, how, and what you're experiencing. Encourage your loved ones to do the same. This keeps you out of your "threat state" and more in your executive/securely attached state.
- **Don't Try to Be Securely Attached to Everyone:** Research shows that you just need a few people in your life that you feel truly safe with in order to reap the mental, physical, and emotional benefits that secure attachment provides.
- **Be Willing to be Vulnerable:** Loving and being in relationship with other flawed human beings is always vulnerable and always a risk. The source of your greatest pain and greatest joy often comes from the messiness of relationships. Secure attachment can only be achieved if both people in the relationship are willing to expose themselves to risk and emotional uncertainty. The risk is high, but the reward is greater.

Write a paragraph or two about your willingness to create secure attachment in your most important relationships as you move forward with your life. What roadblocks do you anticipate? What benefits do you foresee?

____

____

____

____

____

What would "secure attachment" look like in your current relationship(s)? With whom might you practice secure attachment?

Carry the Message to Your Loved Ones

Tracy's life was turned upside down when her husband, Jason, was fired from his pastoral position at their church for inappropriate conduct with a female congregation member. They were immediately shunned and cut off from their church friends and support system at a time when she was most desperate for that connection. Angry, hurt, humiliated, and questioning her entire life and marriage, Tracy sought mental health support. Tracy thought she had a great husband, a great marriage, and that they were raising their three daughters in a healthy way. However, she quickly realized that she barely knew herself, her husband, and her version of God, and she questioned many aspects of her parenting. She felt lost. She committed herself to growth, a better understanding of all that she questioned, and a dedication to raising her three girls in a safe, open way.

Tracy and her husband sought intense couple's and individual therapy to heal from infidelity, betrayal trauma, and childhood trauma while unlearning unhealthy dynamics. They worked hard to heal the hurt and resentment that often build during a marriage. Once they made it through to the other side, they used their story to help others who suffered from similar struggles.

Tracy eventually became a therapist. She specializes in helping women redefine their identity structure, maintain healthy boundaries, and heal trauma wounds. Her husband coaches men, especially men in the church who have struggled with porn use, infidelity, secret-keeping, or leading double lives. Together, Tracy and Jason help other lost women, men, and families, providing support and a healthy path forward. They've created a safe place to turn to when people have been shunned by their support community.

In their personal life, they changed every aspect of how they engage with each other and their family. They have devoted themselves to creating emotionally intelligent children while creating a safe space to share thoughts, feelings, and a better understanding of God, religion, and relationships. They have become champions of healthy boundaries and self-care. They have been able to use their pain and suffering to help others get the empathic, productive help they need during their darkest time.

Many of us have had our own lives turned upside down. We

can't change the past. We can't undo the harm or wrong that's been done. However, study after study shows that our brains can be rewired and wounds can be healed. We can learn healthier coping skills and better ways of interacting with others. We can develop secure connections with others where it's safe for us to disagree, share thoughts and feelings, experience spirituality, and seek help when struggling. All 12 Step work is meant to do this—to allow you to live life on life's terms and to experience healthy connections with others.

One of the greatest signs of mental health is a human who can engage in balanced, honest, fulfilling, intimate relationships with other humans. Ultimately, that is the goal of the 12 Steps.

Terminology: Speaking the Lingo of Recovery

Acting Out: Engaging in behaviors that are not helpful in response to emotional discomfort.

Active Addiction: Delineates between someone who is actively acting out, abusing substances, etc., versus an addict who is in recovery. An addict is always an addict and must always put the time, energy, and commitment into his/her recovery. There is no cure for addiction. There are only active addicts and addicts in recovery.

Al-Anon: A 12-Step program for loved ones of alcoholics.

Amends: A process of apologizing, making things right, and not making the same or similar mistakes in the future.

Attraction, Not Promotion: A term to describe when people *show* others that they've done the work of recovery to heal and grow, versus the need to *espouse* to others how healthy, grounded, and together they are.

Bottom/Rock Bottom: The moment of clarity when an individual realizes that he or she truly has a problem. Usually, this is in the midst of some crisis. This is the moment when the individual realizes he or she is not willing to fall any lower.

Boundaries: Your personal definition of what's OK and not OK with you. Boundaries often complement and are informed by your values and goals.

Character Defects: Usually uncovered in Step 4, character defects are indicative of thinking and behavior that an individual may want to change.

Codependence: An outdated way of looking at loved ones of addicts that says caregiving loved ones tend to partner with addicts because of some inherent shortcoming in themselves—usually driven by unresolved childhood trauma. This model feels blaming and shaming to many loved ones of addicts. (The codependence model is now being replaced by the more positive and affirming prodependence model.)

Denial: A series of internal lies and deceits that eventually manifest externally. The lies that we tell ourselves to justify behaviors that others can clearly see as harmful.

Dry Drunk: A term used to describe an addict who abstains from his or her drug or addictive behavior of choice but doesn't complete 12-Step recovery work or make spiritual, soul-level changes. These people will often be "dry" (without alcohol) but still rage, blame, lie, manipulate, and remain emotionally stunted.

Empathy: The practice of feeling *with* someone, not *for* someone (which is sympathy). Empathy is also a part of the shame resiliency process.

Fake It 'Til You Make It: Individuals sometimes have to begin the process of recovery by making behavioral changes, hoping that those surface changes will eventually develop into deeper, more soulful, longer-lasting changes.

Gaslighting: Gaslighting is a form of psychological abuse that involves the presentation of false information followed by dogged insistence that the information is true.

God-Shaped Wound: This is the same thing as a Hole In the Soul—indicating a need for connection with a Higher Power and others in recovery.

Higher Power: Any power greater than oneself. This does not have to be spiritual or religious in nature, though it often is.

Hit the Pause Button: Often, individuals in recovery struggle to stay in the moment. Instead, they find themselves living in the wreckage of their past or the potential wreckage of their future (which almost never comes to pass). In such cases, they are often told to hit the pause button.

Hole In the Soul: Addicts often say they were trying to fill the hole in their soul with alcohol, drugs, or a behavior, when what they really needed was to connect with a Higher Power and other people.

Interpersonal Attachment: The ability of one human to emotionally attach to another human.

Intimacy: Connecting to self and others in a vulnerable, authentic way. Intimate connection can occur emotionally, physically, intellectually, and spiritually. Intimacy = INTO ME U SEE

In the Rooms: People in 12-Step recovery use this term to describe what goes on in their meetings—what they heard, what they've experienced. What happens in the process of gathering with other people in the recovery process is all stuff that happens "in the rooms."

ISM: Acronym for Incredibly Short Memory.

It Works If You Work It: A saying that is repeated at many 12-Step meetings. "It" refers to the 12 Step program, explaining that you will have success with the program if you put time and effort into connecting with the community and working the steps.

Let Go and Let God: Encouragement to surrender your will and let your Higher Power help you.

Meetings: These are 12-Step meetings, either in-person or online. People who attend meetings are considered to be actively in recovery, more so if they're also working the 12 Steps.

Normies: A term used by addicts to describe non-addicts.

One Day at a Time: A foundational concept to working recovery, emphasizing that individuals should take recovery "one day at a time," focusing on the steps and choices they need to make during that day to stay sober and healthy.

Passive-Aggressive: A type of behavior or characterization where one avoids direct confrontation, communication, or acknowledgment of negative feelings by engaging in indirect, unpleasant acts like sarcasm, lying, blaming others, failing to follow through, or directing hurt or anger at something entirely unrelated.

Play the Tape Forward: A soundbite used to encourage people in recovery to stop, think, and consider the consequences (and potential consequences) before acting or engaging in old, unhealthy behaviors.

Powerlessness: When you've lost control over a behavior. You engage in this behavior even when you say you don't want to do so, and you have no ability to stop the behavior once you've started.

Prodependence: A replacement model for codependence. Prodependence is attachment-based rather than trauma-based. Prodependence celebrates and values a caregiving loved one's willingness to support and stay connected with an addicted family member, while promoting healing for both the individual and the family.

Prodependence Anonymous: A 12 Step program for any person who wants to improve his or her relationships with others.

Progress, Not Perfection: An emphasis on making daily *progress* toward health, healing, and recovery that may come with mistakes and setbacks rather than approaching recovery with "black and white" thinking, where one is only in recovery if one is executing it perfectly.

Recovery: A process of healing, especially when facilitated or helped along by working the 12 Steps.

Resentments: Lingering anger that drives current thinking and behaviors.

Serenity Prayer: "God, grant me the serenity to accept the things I cannot change, the courage to change the things I can, and the wisdom to know the difference." This is a prayer repeated regularly at 12 Step meetings. Participants will often join hands and say it together.

Shame: A deeply rooted fear that one is somehow too broken or "not enough" to be loved, accepted, and valued.

Shame Resilience: The practice of acknowledging, contextualizing, and processing our "shame voices." Sharing our shame with others and experiencing empathy and compassion in response.

Shame Spiral: The act of shameful experiences building upon other shameful experiences. Shame begets more shame if we do not engage in a shame resiliency process.

Shame Voices: The shame-filled, deeply unconscious "stories" and cognitive filters through which we process most of our experiences and realities.

Sobriety Date/Birthday/Anniversary: This is the date of "sobriety" for each addict. Usually, it is celebrated in the rooms each year, mostly as a way of letting newer members know that recovery works and lasting sobriety and healing are possible.

Sponsor: A person in 12-Step recovery who has worked the 12

Steps and is willing to help others work the steps. Sponsors can also provide guidance on simply making it through the day.

Sponsee: A person new to 12-Step recovery who wants to work the 12 Steps and asks a sponsor to guide that process. Sponsees may also ask a sponsor for guidance on day-to-day living.

Stinking Thinking: Shame-based thinking that leads addicts and others into behaviors that do not match their values, goals, and desired way of living.

Trauma: Generally speaking, trauma (victimization and abuse) is defined as any event or experience (including witnessing) that is physically and/or psychologically overwhelming in the moment or later (when the event is remembered). Trauma is highly subjective, meaning incidents that are highly traumatic to one person might not be traumatic for another.

Unmanageability: Life is unmanageable when an individual experiences consequences related to behaviors over which he or she is powerless.

Vulnerability: Exposure to risk, harm, and emotional uncertainty.

White-Knuckling: A term used to describe an addict who has abstained from their addictive behavior or substance out of "sheer will and desire" rather than humbling themselves and surrendering to the 12-Step recovery process. This type of abstinence is usually short-term, as its only more of an addict's attempt to assert control rather than give up control.

You Spot It, You Got It: The idea that if you notice a behavior or a pattern or a struggle in someone else's story/experience, it most likely stuck out to you because you have struggled in a similar way.

Recommended Reading

A New Pair of Glasses, by Charles A. Chamberlain

Attached: The New Science of Adult Attachment and How it Can Help You Find—and Keep—Love, by Amir Levine, MD and Rachel S.F. Heller, MA

The Body Keeps the Score: Brain, Mind, and Body in the Healing of Trauma, by Bessel van der Kolk, MD

Breathing Under Water: Spirituality and the Twelve Steps, by Richard Rohr

Courageous Love: A Couples Guide to Conquering Betrayal, by Stefanie Carnes, PhD

Daring Greatly: How the Courage to Be Vulnerable Transforms the Way We Live, Love, Parent, and Lead, by Brené Brown PhD, LCSW

The Gaslight Effect: How to Spot and Survive the Hidden Manipulation Others Use to Control Your Life, by Robin Stern

A Gentle Path through the Twelve Steps: A Guide for All People in the Process of Recovery, by Dr. Patrick Carnes

In the Realm of Hungry Ghosts: Close Encounters with Addiction, by Gabor Maté

I Thought It Was Just Me (But It Isn't), by Brené Brown PhD, LCSW

A Man's Way through the Twelve Steps, by Dan Griffin, MA

The Mindful Self-Compassion Workbook: A Proven Way to Accept Yourself, Build Inner Strength, and Thrive, by Kristin Neff, PhD and Christopher Germer, PhD

Neglect: The Silent Abuser, by Enod Gray

Pastrix: The Cranky, Beautiful Faith of a Sinner & Saint, by Nadia Bolz-Weber

Paths to Recovery: Al-Anon's Steps, Traditions, and Concepts, by Al-Anon's Family Group

The Polyvagal Theory: Neurophysiological Foundations of Emotions, Attachment, Communication, and Self-Regulation, by Stephen W. Porges

Prodependence: Moving Beyond Codependency, by Robert Weiss, PhD

The Power of Showing Up: How Parental Presence Shapes Who Our Kids Become and How Their Brains Get Wired, by Daniel J Siegal, MD and Tina Payne Bryson, PhD

Rising Strong: How the Ability to Reset Transforms the Way We Live, Love, Parent, and Lead, by Brené Brown PhD, LCSW

Surviving Disclosure: A Partner's Guide for Healing and the Betrayal of Intimate Trust, by Dr. M. Deborah Corley and Dr. Jennifer Schneider

The Twelve Steps and Twelve Traditions, by Alcoholics Anonymous

The Ultimate Survival Guide for Navigating Healthy Boundaries, by Deborah DePolo MA, LPC

Waking the Tiger: Healing Trauma, by Peter A. Levine

A Woman's Way through the Twelve Steps, by Dr. Stephanie Covington

Author Biographies

Kristin M. Snowden MA, LMFT #81413

Kristin Snowden, MA, is a licensed marriage and family therapist and certified life coach in Thousand Oaks, California. In addition to maintaining a private practice, Kristin is the Sex and Love Addiction Specialist and Adjunct Therapist at Avalon Malibu, a treatment center for substance abuse and mental health disorders. She is also a writer and webinar host for Sex and Relationship Healing, a free online resource for people struggling with intimacy disorders, addictions, and relationship crises (i.e., sex/porn addiction, infidelity, and betrayal trauma). Kristin previously helped develop and run the SAID (Substance Abuse & Intimacy Disorders) Program at Promises Malibu under Dr. Rob Weiss. The men's only drug and sex addiction program was the first of its kind in the world. Highlighting the impor-tance of comprehensive, multi-focused addiction treatment with additional support for betrayed partners. Kristin is a Certified Daring Way® Facilitator, based on Dr. Brené Brown's research. She believes in the integration of neuroscience, trauma treatment, attachment theory, and 12 Steps recovery. Healing can come from safe connection, vulnerability, and shame resiliency. Kristin holds an honors undergraduate degree from the University of Southern California and a Master's degree in Psychology from Chapman University. Kristin regularly hosts webinars, workshops, and educational lectures. She has been married for nearly 20 years and has three young children. www.KristinSnowden.com.

Scott Brassart JD, MA

Scott Brassart is a writer, editor, and content creator. He is the author of *Sex and Porn Addiction Healing and Recovery: A Practical Daily Reader for Sex and Porn Addicts*. As Director of Content Development for Seeking Integrity LLC, he oversees the creation, production, and dissemination of all written content, both online and print, including blogs, social media, treatment manuals, newsletters, press releases, brochures, etc. For the websites SeekingIntegrity.com and SexandRelationshipHealing.com, he creates original content and works with outside contributors. He is also a long-recovering sex and substance addict.

A graduate of Brown University (BA), Emerson College (MA), and Indiana University School of Law (JD), Scott has been a writer and editor for more than 25 years. He has worked closely with Dr. Robert Weiss for the past ten years, creating treatment manuals, writing and posting blogs, editing books, helping to create educational presentations for speaking engagements, crafting scholarly and popular articles, and more. He has helped Dr. Rob develop both a significant social media presence and a significant online readership (19 million hits on Psychology Today alone).

As an individual whose life was once controlled and nearly destroyed by sex and substance addiction, Scott is passionate about helping others to recover and heal as he has done. To this end, his sole writing focus for the last decade has been on mental health and addiction-related topics, especially sex and porn addiction. In addition to his work with Dr. Rob, he has worked with Dr. David Fawcett, Dr. Pat Carnes, Dr. Stefanie Carnes, Dr. Jennifer Schneider, and numerous other highly regarded clinicians and educators.

Made in the USA
Middletown, DE
24 March 2021